Henry Wylde

Severed ties

Vol. III

Henry Wylde

Severed ties
Vol. III

ISBN/EAN: 9783337040567

Printed in Europe, USA, Canada, Australia, Japan

Cover: Foto ©ninafisch / pixelio.de

More available books at **www.hansebooks.com**

SEVERED TIES.

BY
MRS. HENRY WYLDE.

IN THREE VOLUMES.

VOL. III.

LONDON:
F. V. WHITE & CO.,
31, SOUTHAMPTON STREET, STRAND, W.C.
1889.

PRINTED BY
KELLY & CO., GATE STREET, LINCOLN'S INN FIELDS,
AND KINGSTON-ON-THAMES.

CONTENTS.

CHAP.		PAGE
I.—Stop Thief!		1
II.—The Berwick Attorney		29
III.—The Right Man at Last		37
IV.—The Jesuit's Threat		54
V.—The Shipwreck		67
VI.—Discovery of the Robbery		86
VII.—Sir Charles Leslie Stood Before Them		113
VIII.—Sick Unto Death		130
IX.—Varani and his Son		145
X.—The Honourable George		154
XI.—How dare you, Villain, Use my Mother's Name?		181
XII.—My Child! My Child!		210
XIII.—Halt! or I Fire		227
XIV.—The Last Hour		235

SEVERED TIES.

POPULAR NEW NOVELS.

Now Ready, the Seventh Edition of

ARMY SOCIETY. By JOHN STRANGE WINTER, Author of "Bootles' Baby." Cloth gilt, 6s.; also picture boards, 2s.

Also, now Ready, in Cloth Gilt, 2s. 6d. each.

GARRISON GOSSIP, Gathered in Blankhampton. By JOHN STRANGE WINTER. Also picture boards, 2s.

A SIEGE BABY. By the same AUTHOR. Also picture boards, 2s.

IN THE SHIRES. By SIR RANDAL H. ROBERTS, Bart.

THE GIRL IN THE BROWN HABIT. A Sporting Novel. By Mrs. EDWARD KENNARD. Also picture boards, 2s.

BY WOMAN'S WIT. By Mrs. ALEXANDER, Author of "The Wooing O't." Also picture boards, 2s.

MONA'S CHOICE. By the same AUTHOR.

KILLED IN THE OPEN. By Mrs. EDWARD KENNARD. Also picture boards, 2s.

IN A GRASS COUNTRY. By Mrs. H. LOVETT-CAMERON. Also picture boards, 2s.

A DEVOUT LOVER. By the same AUTHOR.

THE COST OF A LIE. By the same AUTHOR.

THE OUTSIDER. By HAWLEY SMART. Also picture boards, 2s.

STRAIGHT AS A DIE. By Mrs. EDWARD KENNARD. Also picture boards, 2s.

TWILIGHT TALES. By Mrs. EDWARD KENNARD. Illustrated.

SHE CAME BETWEEN. By Mrs. ALEXANDER FRASER.

THE CRUSADE OF THE "EXCELSIOR." By BRET HARTE. Also picture boards, 2s.

CURB AND SNAFFLE. By SIR RANDAL H. ROBERTS, Bart

A REAL GOOD THING. By Mrs. EDWARD KENNARD. Also picture boards, 2s.

A CRACK COUNTY. By the same AUTHOR.

DREAM FACES. By THE HONBLE. MRS. FETHERSTONHAUGH. Also picture boards, 2s.

THE HONBLE. MRS. VEREKER. By the Author of "Molly Bawn," &c.

**F. V. WHITE & CO.,
31, Southampton Street, Strand, London, W.C.**

SEVERED TIES.

CHAPTER I.

STOP THIEF!

Mr. Morton's mansion in Belgrave Square looked gloomy and untenanted, as Tom let himself in with his latch key, and repaired instantly to the library, where some slight preparation had been made for him by the old woman left in charge. A silver tray containing a large plate of sandwiches, some biscuits, and fruit, was placed on the table, whilst glasses, decanters of wine, and an unopened champagne bottle with syphons of soda and seltzer water, stood invitingly around. Tom glanced quickly about the room to see if all were in order for his expected guest, and then ran upstairs. Taking the key of the large back drawing-room from his pocket, he entered the room in which all poor Dora's wedding presents had been locked up, after the dreadful catastrophe that had occurred. Tom determined to return all to their respective donors; and to achieve this onerous and unpleasant task, Meg had been pressed into the service, and had promised to spend the evening with him, and help to pack up and send off the pretty baubles.

Traces of the festivity that had so suddenly been put an end to, were still about the house. Fragments of crimson cloth, where a large balcony had been covered in, chairs and tables piled up in a closet to make more room for the expected guests, that void, desolate look, generally seen in a big house after a large party, and more than usually visible to-night, as the servants had been busily packing all day, having no time to attend to their ordinary work. Mr. Morton and Dolly had started for Loombe by the early morning express, and now the last detachment of servants, and luggage, had just departed, all having been superintended by Tom, who had just seen the carriages, horses, and attendants safely off from King's Cross station, and had now returned for a long evening's unpleasant work, but which he knew would be brightened, and made endurable, by Meg's sweet presence. And sure enough, as Tom, having strolled listlessly through the rooms, looked out at the window on to the square, he quickly spied his lady love tripping lightly across ; and forgetting all else, save the charm of again beholding her pretty face, down he rushed, and arrived at the entrance in time to admit her.

"My darling," said Tom, as he closed the door, and placed an arm round her waist, drawing her to him and tenderly kissing her, "how I have longed for your arrival! I have had a most painful business all day, and sadly want my Meg to soothe and comfort me."

"Well, here I am, dear," replied the girl, "and now we must set to work, for it is past seven, and I must not stay later than ten. I am very uneasy about dear Lady Leslie; she seems to get weaker and thinner every day, and the doctor here looked grave this morning, and bade me be very careful of her, saying, the sooner we left London the better."

"I thought she seemed ill, and out of spirits, yesterday, as if something were preying on her mind. Is she happy, Meg? Sir Charles seems a good sort of old fellow, but his wife always gives me the impression that she is afraid of him. Tell me, was it originally a love match? He is so many years older than she is; *I* have not much faith in a marriage turning out happily where there is so great a disparity of age."

"Now, dear Tom," said Meg, " you must not ask me anything about Lady Leslie, or

Sir Charles either, because it would not be right for me to tell you. I am very fond of Lady Leslie, and am deeply sorry for her, though I like Sir Charles also, for he has always been good and kind to me, and I'm sure he wishes to do his duty, and make his wife happy, but there is no denying, he is too old for her, and unsuited in many respects. Just now, I am most grieved about her health, and am very anxious."

"But when we get to Loombe, you *will* leave her, and let us be married, won't you darling? You ought to think a little of me too, ducky," said Tom, jealously, "and remember how I long to call you my own, and take you off to our Lancashire home. I can't live much longer without my Meg, and now it will be worse than ever, for I have been too much away lately, as it is, from the Factory, and expect I shall have to stick to it a bit now."

"Dear old boy," said Meg, lovingly, throwing an arm round his neck and laying her head on his shoulder, " I am as anxious as you are for our wedding, and now that your father has consented, and my old people know of it, there is no cause for delay, excepting Lady Leslie, but I am at a loss to know what to do about her. Directly I proposed leaving, she began to cry, and, as I told you, begged me so earnestly not to desert her, that I hadn't the heart to refuse, and now that she is so ill and weak, I positively *dare* not mention the subject."

"But we can't go on for ever like this," said Tom, impatiently; "if you won't tell her, lass, why *I* shall. I'm sure if she only knew the facts of the case, she wouldn't be so hard on us. I'll just tell her, and Sir Charles too."

"No, no, Tom, anyhow, wait awhile; perhaps when we get to Loombe, she may be better, and then I'll confess all the truth. She is so kind to me, that I know she'll forgive me."

During this conversation, the packing had been going on vigorously. Presents of plate, jewellery, Dresden china, statues, needlework, knick-knacks of all kinds, inkstands, vases, etc., were put into their respective cases, ready to be returned to their donors, Tom addressing them all, and undertaking to provide a messenger to leave them at the different houses the next day. Then Meg and her lover repaired to the library, and had supper, Tom opening the bottle of champagne, and drinking to the health of his darling, and to their speedy marriage. Time seems to fly when lovers meet, and Tom declared they *could* never have been together more than an hour, when the clock struck ten, and Meg said she must go. Young Morton insisted on seeing her home, so a cab was called, and they drove off happily together. On reaching the Regent's Park, Tom, anxious to delay parting with his companion, proposed that, as the night was so warm and fine, they should descend, and walk to the house, so giving his arm to Meg, the two strolled slowly and contentedly together till the garden entrance to the Leslies' villa could be seen in the distance. As Meg paused, to say a few last words, the gate softly opened, and a tall dark man, carrying what looked like a bundle of rope, came out, and quickly passed them. Meg, who caught sight of his face, although he evidently wished to shun observation, gave a violent start, and with a low cry, clung closer to her lover's arm, as the latter, with a bound backwards, seized the intruder by the arm, and held him in an iron grasp, whilst he sternly demanded what business he had there, and by what right he had entered the garden from which they had just beheld his exit.

Varani, struggling to free himself from the strong hand that held him, explained that he was a friend of the valet, lately come over from Italy, and had called to see him, whereupon Giuseppe, who had just parted with his brother, came out, and corroborated this story, so that honest Tom reluctantly removed his hand, and allowed the Count to pass. Giuseppe then, after a good stare at Meg, humbly said "Good night, sir," to Tom, and discreetly re-entered the garden, leaving the lovers to say farewell undisturbed.

"Now, Meg, darling," began Tom, "you must tell Lady Leslie directly of our attachment, for that Italian rascal will be sure to chatter, and then it will be unpleasant for you, but what on earth's the matter?" he added, as he looked at Meg, and noticed she had turned deadly pale, whilst her eyes had a terrified expression, and she trembled violently.

"Oh, Tom," gasped Meg, "I *am* so frightened. That dreadful man alive and here!"

"What dreadful man? Do you know him then? Now, Meg, look here," said

Tom, more sternly than he had ever spoken to the girl before, "this won't do! If you've had one of those Italian rascals making up to you over there, I'll be shot if he shall come here after you."

"Nonsense, Tom," said Meg, trying hard to recover herself, "he doesn't come after me, no fear!"

"It's all very fine to say 'Nonsense, Tom,' but I won't have it! I insist on knowing who the man is, and all about it."

"That is just what I cannot tell you, dear," said Meg, "but I give you my solemn assurance that he is nothing to me, and never has been."

"Ah, Meg,' said Tom, reproachfully, "I didn't think this of you! If the man was nothing to you, why did you turn pale, and be so upset, at the sight of him? If you've had a sweetheart, child, tell me the truth at once, and have done with it. I know my Meg never did anything to blush for, and I've no wish to enquire too closely about any little past flirtations, but when you show such terror at the sight of a man I never saw or heard of before, I've a right to enquire who he is, and I repeat, I insist on knowing."

"Dear Tom," said Meg earnestly, "pray believe me, and ask no more. It would be wrong and dishonourable of me were I to tell you. The man does not come after me. Look in my eyes, and read in them, that I speak truly, and never doubt me again. I love you, and will never deceive you."

"Well, lass," said Tom reluctantly, "I don't wish to doubt you when you speak like that, but it's not beginning well; I'm your lover, and hope soon to be your husband; I've no secrets from you, Meg, and I don't consider you *ought* to have any from me."

"And I never will in future, Tom," replied Meg, looking lovingly at him, as she pressed his hand to her heart, "but this, dear, does not concern me, and I must not, I dare not, tell you."

"Very well, Meg, I trust you, but mind, I don't like it! And what's more, I don't think you are right. How can we be happy, if we have not perfect confidence in each other? Believe me, lass, that what you can't tell your husband must be wrong, and will surely get you into trouble some day."

"Oh, Tom," said Meg, with tears in her

eyes, "don't worry me, dear, just now! Indeed, I am so unhappy and uneasy that I would give anything to be able to tell you, and ask you what to do. Pray don't be vexed with me, or think that I *wish* to keep anything from you. Will you be satisfied if I tell you, that the man we have just seen, is an enemy to Sir Charles Leslie, and that I intend going straight to Lady Leslie, and warning her that he is in England, directly I leave you?"

"Ah!" said Tom, starting, "that alters the case! Sir Charles mixed up with it, is he? Then, darling, I won't ask more. Forgive me for teasing you; only remember that if ever you want help or advice, that Tom Morton will give you the best in his power, and never betray the trust and confidence you, or anyone you care for, repose in him."

So saying they parted, and Meg ran in, took off her bonnet, and tried to collect her thoughts, and regain her self-possession before seeing her mistress, for she knew that the interview would be both painful and trying; but the honest girl felt that for the happiness and welfare of all concerned she was bound to speak, and she determined—much as she liked Lady Leslie—that if the *liaison* with Count Varani was again renewed, that she would leave at once. How could she, in honour to Tom Morton, delay her marriage, and get mixed up in an affair that could only end scandalously and unhappily?

Meg was thoroughly honest and straightforward, and felt she could not lead a life of deceit and disguise to Sir Charles and to her dear Tom, and although she was deeply attached to Lady Leslie, and truly sorry for her, she would not aid and abet in again deceiving the husband, who had shown such noble generosity and Christian forbearance, and mercy towards his wife.

Lightly, Meg tripped upstairs, and entered the dressing-room adjoining Lady Leslie's bed-room, where she slept. All was quiet, but the girl could see that lights were still burning in the bed-room. She gently pushed the door half open and peeped in, to find Leonora just regaining consciousness, but still terribly prostrated. On seeing Meg she burst into tears and threw her arms round the faithful girl's neck, begging her never again to leave her.

"Oh, milady," said the girl, "how distressed I am to see you suffer! What can I do? Shall I call Sir Charles?"

"Oh, no!" replied Lady Leslie; "indeed, Meg, you must not tell him you found me so upset. It could do no good, and would only worry him."

"Milady." said Meg gravely, "I know why you are so miserable; Count Varani is not dead, as we thought; he has been here; I know it, for I met him at the garden gate."

"Oh, Meg," cried Leonora, frightened, and hiding her face as if ashamed, "I hope no one else saw him!"

"I know not, Lady Leslie," said the girl, "but he must not come here and bring fresh misery and disgrace to you. Ah! you were very wrong to admit him."

"Do you suppose I saw him willingly, Meg? Indeed, indeed, it was not my fault. How he came here, I know not, or how he managed to gain admittance to my room. I was feeling very ill, and came upstairs instead of going in to dinner; I knelt for some time praying, as usual, when to my horror and consternation he suddenly appeared from behind a curtain."

"Ah, dear Lady," said Meg, "surely you did not let him stay? You ought to have sent him away instantly. Now you *must* tell Sir Charles at once. Did you not promise to have no more secrets from him?"

"Dear Meg," said Lady Leslie, "have patience with me, and do not fear that I shall again fall, or give you cause to blame me. I told Count Varani that nothing would induce me to listen to him, and at last he consented to abide by my decision."

"I am glad to hear it," replied the girl, "but still I think Sir Charles ought to be told."

"Ah, no!" sighed Lady Leslie, "anyhow, not at present. Promise me, Meg, that you will say nothing; at least let Varani have time to leave England, and then I will tell my husband everything."

"But how is it milady, that the valet Giuseppe, knows Count Varani?"

"What!" said Lady Leslie, horrified. "Giuseppe knows Count Varani? Impossible! What can you mean?"

"Giuseppe was with the Count to-night, and let him out of the garden gate. He told Tom Morton that he was a friend of his," said Meg.

"How Count Varani managed to get in here unobserved, I know not," replied Leonora. "He was so upset at finding me so ill, and I so distressed at seeing him, and so anxious to send him away, that we had very little conversation; he certainly never told me he knew Giuseppe."

"I don't like the look of it," said Meg seriously. "Sir Charles must send away Giuseppe, and the sooner the better; he is evidently paid by Count Varani.

"I cannot believe that," said Lady Leslie, "but I promise you that at the end of next week, I will confide all to Sir Charles, and then you may tell him all you know, and leave him to decide what is best to be done."

Not even to her faithful companion did Lady Leslie mention the promise she had given Varani, of seeing him once more, and trusting her little child to his care. She had determined, for Paolo's sake, to make this ·sacrifice, and would not run the risk of being prevented from accomplishing it. Meg still felt uneasy and suspicious, but did not dare say more, and the girl had her own troubles and anxieties. She thought the valet might mention the fact of her being out with Tom Morton, and dreaded the probable questions and remarks that would be made amongst the tenants and domestics. To-night she felt, more than ever, that she was in a false position, and had no right to degrade her wealthy lover by remaining in her present position, whilst engaged to him. She longed intensely to be married, and away, safely, with Tom; for ever removed from the tittle-tattle and petty jealousies she had to put up with, as humble companion; yet she was deeply attached to Lady Leslie, and had for long been treated by her more as a friend than an attendant. When she was a child, Sir Charles Leslie (who so highly valued her old parents) had taken a great fancy to their pretty little daughter, and had given her a better education than was enjoyed by most of her class, and the girl had always felt under a deep debt of gratitude to him, although his naturally cold, stern manner, slightly repulsed her, and her sympathies were more strongly enlisted in his wife's favour, as she gradually learnt her history, and felt how much she was to be pitied. So, of late years, Meg had been torn by conflicting emotions; affection and compassion for the wife; gratitude and respect for the husband; yet hitherto she had managed to steer the middle course, and had remained faithful and true to both. Now, after bringing her mistress wine and cakes, and tenderly trying to persuade her to eat, Meg knelt before her, and hiding her head in her lap, said: "Dear Lady Leslie, forgive me if I pain you, but I cannot, I dare not, longer conceal the truth from you. I shall be obliged to leave you, though it grieves me sadly, whilst you are so ill and unhappy, but I am going to be married, and the person I am engaged to objects to my remaining longer in the position I now occupy."

"Dear Meg," said Leonora kindly, as she kissed the girl, and made her sit beside her, " you astonish me ! Why did you not tell me, and ask my advice, before engaging yourself? Do your parents know of it? Has the man a respectable position, and enough to give you a comfortable home? And, above all, do you really love him?"

"Ah, Milady," replied Meg, " all I fear is, that he is too good for me; he is certainly above me in station, and he is a wealthy man, but we love each other dearly, and his old father knows all about it, and has forgiven him, and promised to love and be kind to me." So saying, Meg confided all to Lady Leslie, and told her in conclusion, that as the Italian valet had seen Tom with her that evening, she felt bound to tell her and Sir Charles without further delay. Leonora was greatly astonished, but warmly congratulated Meg on her good fortune, in having secured such an honourable, good-hearted young fellow for a husband, and deeply as she regretted parting with her faithful friend, she felt it would be cruel and unjust to keep her longer in the humble position she at present occupied, whilst her lover impatiently waited to give her his name, and take her to his Lancashire home. So it was arranged that, soon after they returned to Loombe, Meg should be quietly married at the village church, so that her old parents, Mr. Morton, and Lady Leslie might be present, and that a daughter of one of the tenants on the estate, that had often been at the Manor, and had received a good education, should be engaged immediately, so that Meg might instruct her a little before leaving. Leonora felt bitterly the approaching loss of her kind companion, and when she had dismissed her for the night, the thought of this added greatly to her other sorrows. Misfortune and grief seemed to be gathering thicker and thicker around her, from which there was no escape, no hope, save in death. She felt too nervous, too excited to sleep, or even retain a recumbent posture; and sat by the open window, breathing the warm, balmy air of the June night, counting the slow minutes, and watching till the sun mounted the heavens.

In such vigils as Leonora had of late, too often kept, life wastes quickly; vigils in which the mind, having no pleasant thoughts to nourish it, no manna of hope, endeavours to exist on philosophy, on resignation.

Leonora prayed earnestly for strength; for relief; but we all know, this world is the scene of trial and probation, and instead of any favourable change, resulting from her prayers, it appeared to her, they were neither listened to or accepted.

CHAPTER II.

THE BERWICK ATTORNEY.

"I say it serves them jolly well right," said old Mrs. Smith, throwing down the newspaper, after reading an elaborate account of the terrible fiasco at poor Dolly's intended wedding, and glancing across the table at her son as she carefully wiped her spectacles and restored them to their case. "After the way Dora Morton treated you last winter she deserves to be punished, and I for one don't pity her. A stuck-up, deceitful little minx!"

"Don't be too hard, mother. Depend

upon it poor Dolly has suffered enough, without your reproaching her. I am thankful she is spared the wretched life she would have passed as Lord Booby's wife, for he must be a bad lot, from all I hear of him."

So said young John Smith, who had just entered the little front parlour, the window of which, carefully shrouded by a wire blind, looked on to the High Street at Berwick, and was the special sanctum of the old attorney's wife, who preferred living in this small den near the office, in which her husband and son passed their days, to inhabiting the large, gloomy drawing-room on the first floor.

The Smiths were of humble but respectable origin, and dwelt in a large red-brick house in the heart of the town of Berwick;

a house having a straight row of small windows, all having neat wire blinds on the ground floor, and above, prim chintz curtains, that looked more intended for show than comfort.

A large, brightly polished, brass plate shone on the door, on which was engraved " John Smith and Son "—Solicitors!

Business had not been too prosperous of late years, for the good folk of Berwick seemed to prefer settling their little quarrels and litigations privately and amicably, to falling into the lawyer's hands, though old Smith was an honest, upright man, and never advised his clients to enter a law-suit that would probably be detrimental to their interests, for the sake of his own share of the spoils. He was a wizened, grey-haired little man, about sixty-five, with keen black eyes, and a slim, wiry form, and his son, though only thirty, closely resembled him. The same dapper little figure, and bright piercing eyes, only his hair was a dark brown, and his complexion clearer, and without the lines and wrinkles that time and care had unsparingly bestowed on the father. This was the man who last Christmas had wooed and nearly won Miss Dora; for the girl had grown to like him, and would have listened to his suit, and saved herself the pain and disgrace she had lately undergone, had not her foolish pride and vanity whispered that she ought to make a better match, and with her fortune marry into the nobility! Now, she deeply regretted young Smith, who, though pecuniary interests and the hope of rising in his profession by a wealthy marriage, had, we must confess, originally prompted to make up to the cotton spinner's daughter, yet was a straightforward, good-hearted young fellow, and would make a kind and faithful husband, if a somewhat stolid and unromantic one. The idea quickly flashed across his mind that perhaps Miss Dora might now not be quite so unapproachable, and might be pleased to turn a willing ear to a suitor more in her own station of life. Surely, he soliloquised, she's had enough of lords, and will be glad to console herself with a good respectable middle-class husband, especially as young Smith remembered certain tender passages and flirtations that had passed between them; so he determined to say nothing at present to the old folk, but to try his luck once more with the plump, rosy Dora.

It so happened that Mr. Morton, who had placed all business matters connected with his large estate at Loombe in the hands of the Berwick solicitor, wanted to see him about a refractory tenant, so determined to stay a night with his daughter at the Hotel, and take the opportunity of calling at Mr. Smith's office before returning to the Castle.

Accordingly, early the next morning, he was closeted with the old attorney, young John Smith having gone out on another client's business, at the further end of the town.

Miss Dora, who still suffered too deeply from mortification, and wounded pride and vanity, to care to pay visits to any of her friends in the country town, or even to accompany her father to the solicitors office, strolled leisurely down the High Street during the old man's absence, listlessly and discontentedly, looking in at the shop windows, and regretting the loss of the high position she had so greatly coveted, and that had been, at the last moment, as it were, snatched from her grasp. Then her thoughts strayed to John Smith, and she wondered if he ever now remembered her, and if he would be sorry for her, or rejoice at the *contretemps* that had so unexpectedly set her free.

Meanwhile John Smith, not having the least idea that Miss Dora and her father were in Berwick, had hurriedly left the office to keep an appointment, and was rushing along the street, in his usual impetuous manner, when he actually ran up against his former lady love, without for the moment recognising her through the thick veil she wore to conceal her red eyes and tear-stained cheeks from the vulgar gaze.

"Beg pardon, Ma'am! Why, it's Miss Morton!" ejaculated Smith, hastily doffing his hat, as he shook hands with the girl. An awkward pause ensued, for they had not met since the young lawyer had proffered his suit to Miss Dora, and been so ignominiously repulsed, and he felt half afraid to mention the *contretemps* that had occurred at the intended wedding, lest he might hurt or wound the girl's feelings. Ultimately Dora herself spoke of it, saying she had had a lucky escape, and then they chatted pleasantly and amicably together, and Smith received and accepted an invitation to call shortly at the Castle.

CHAPTER III.

THE RIGHT MAN AT LAST.

Kind Dr. Grey was greatly shocked at the change six weeks had wrought in Lady Leslie, when he met the family at the Station at Loombe on their arrival, neither did the poor old man feel happy and satisfied about his little daughter, who, he thought, looked pale and thin, and not so merry and joyous as three months' ago, though she assured him she was well and happy.

"Why, Ellen," he ejaculated, "what mischief this London season has done! *You* have lost all the roses from your cheeks, but Lady Leslie positively alarms me. I couldn't have believed any woman could have changed so terribly in such a short time! What can be the matter with her?"

"The doctors fear consumption," said Ellen, gravely, "and Sir Charles is very uneasy, for he knows her father died of it."

Dr. Grey had heard from the Baronet of his son's unsuccessful suit, and of young Meredith's attachment, but refrained from mentioning the subject to his child, wishing to leave her entirely unbiassed in the matter. He knew nothing of Frank, having only seen him that one evening at the Manor, and was secretly much distressed and disappointed, that his darling should have refused Tony, who would have been the husband after his own heart for her, and given her such a high position. But no worldly consideration could induce the good Vicar to say a word to influence his child in a choice that would bring either happiness, or sorrow, to her whole young life, and so things remained, and the quiet, peaceful life was resumed between father and daughter, until a few days later the young barrister arrived at Loombe, as a guest at the Manor. Tony had stayed in London with his aunt, Lady Harman, and it had been arranged that he should accompany her and her young sisters, to Switzerland, on an autumnal tour, only returning to Loombe for a few days, to see his parents before starting; for the boy still suffered from Ellen's refusal, and Sir Charles was too well versed in human nature, not to be aware that a change of scene, and absence from the loved object, would soon, at Tony's age, cure him of a hopeless attachment. So when Frank Meredith appeared at the northern village, there was nothing to prevent his showing attention and respect to Dr. Grey and his pretty daughter, and gradually allowing the latter to perceive the love and admiration she had excited in his heart. He soon ingratiated himself into the favour of the kind old Vicar, who admired his straightforward, honest manner, and high principles, and felt that though, in a worldly point of view, he would not be so good a match for his child as the Baronet's son, that he would feel after all, easier and safer, in trusting her happiness to *his* care, than to that of the passionate, quick-tempered, half Italian boy he had loved for his father's sake.

So when Frank confided to Dr. Grey the

attachment he felt for Ellen, explained his present position, and the hopes he had of soon being able to offer her a suitable and comfortable home, the old man assented, though he felt what a loss he would sustain when his darling should be taken from him.

A week had now elapsed since the Leslies' return to Loombe, but as yet, Meredith had abstained from speaking openly to Ellen, or pressing his suit, being anxious, if possible, to win the young girl's affection and confidence, before risking the question that would decide his fate.

It was a bright sunny afternoon, towards the end of July, when Ellen, after kissing her father, and promising to be back in time for dinner, ran gaily out of the house to repair to the Manor, to enquire after Lady Leslie, whose failing health caused the greatest anxiety and apprehension to all around her. Ellen had first to visit a sick parishioner, so went round by the village, determining to take a short cut from thence to the Baronet's.

Frank Meredith, who had dined at the Vicarage the previous evening, had learnt from Ellen of her intended afternoon excursion, and waylaid her as she turned from the village, up the steep ascent that led to the Manor. "Good afternoon, Miss Grey," said the young barrister, shaking hands, and bending his soft grey eyes tenderly on her, "may I accompany you?"

"With pleasure," said Ellen, blushing, and looking down to avoid the young man's impassioned gaze, though she allowed him to persuade her to take the longer and less steep pathway, which wound round the brow of the hill, and would thus give time for half-an-hour's conversation. They talked first of Lady Leslie's health, and Ellen said, how uneasy and unhappy they all were about her; Meredith looked grave, and acknowledged that he thought her terribly altered, and that *he* feared consumption.

"Oh!" said Ellen, with tears in her eyes, "how grieved I should be if anything happened to her; she is so kind and good to me and all around her, so gentle and affectionate to her boys; I am sure the patience she has with little Luigi, is marvellous, for he *is* a naughty child, and I know, at times, makes his mother very unhappy.'

"A dreadful boy!" exclaimed Frank, shuddering. "So unlike my dear friend

Tony, who, though quick tempered, is honest and open as the day. It is hard to believe they are brothers, for there is not one similar trait in their characters."

"No, indeed," said Ellen. "Tony is a dear, good-hearted boy, and universally beloved; so affectionate to his parents, and kind to the servants, and tenants, in the estate."

"And yet Miss Grey could not love him, and look kindly on his suit," said Meredith, glancing searchingly at the girl, who coloured deeply, and cast her eyes on the ground. "Yes," he added, "Tony told me all about it. Miss Grey, do you remember how upset he was the night of Mr. Morton's ball, because we danced so much together?"

"Oh, no!" said Ellen nervously.

"Surely that could not have been the reason. I do remember that Tony was cross, and I never could understand why. He would not tell me, though I asked him."

"It was in consequence of what he said that night, that I left the next day, and saw so little of you in London. Sir Charles Leslie had been so kind to me·that I could not go against his son, and strive to accomplish the dearest wish of my heart at his expense; but I did not dare trust myself to see more of you. I suffered deeply, but I felt it would be dishonourable and useless for me, a poor barrister, to enter the lists against the rich baronet's son, a marriage with whom would please the parents on both sides, and give you the noble position that you would grace so well." Then, as

Ellen remained silent, the young barrister continued :

"But now that Tony tells me he has abandoned all hope, my lips are no longer sealed.

"Oh, Miss Grey! Ellen!" he cried, taking her unresisting hand, "from the first day we met I loved you; life to me without you, is a blank. I cannot, dare not, hope that I have as yet made any impression on you; but will you try to love me a little?

"Look up, darling," he added, as the girl's head drooped lower and lower, and the tears gathered in her eyes; "look up, and tell me you forgive my presumption in thus addressing you; give me some slight hope, some sign that you are not displeased with me?"

But Ellen could not raise her head; the tears flowed down her cheeks, and a deep sob escaped her; but her hand remained unresistingly in Frank's grasp, and she did not shrink from the arm that stole lovingly around her.

"Dear Ellen," said the young man, as he led her to a fallen tree that offered a rustic seat by the pathway, "speak to me; tell me that I am not indifferent to you?"

"But my father!" murmured the girl, half inaudibly.

"Your father, dearest, knows I love you, and has allowed me to speak to you! Oh, Ellen," said Frank rapturously, "I begin to feel that my love is not in vain; that you almost care for me!"

Then, as the young girl timidly raised her eyes to his, and he saw the love that even her innate modesty could not prevent shining from them, he strained her closer to his heart, and, bending tenderly over her, implanted a long, fervent kiss on the innocent lips that no man, save her old father, had ever before touched. He gradually drew from the girl the confession that she had long loved him, and that his coldness and avoidance of her had deeply wounded her; that she had tried hard to conquer the affection he had aroused in her breast, and her pride and self-respect had enabled her to disguise all she suffered, when she imagined that Frank had only flirted with her on the night of Mr. Morton's ball, and that now he studiously shunned her, and tried to show her that he had no serious intentions.

At last Frank Meredith knew that the

pale cheek and languid health were caused by sorrow at his seeming coldness; that the listless indifference to the gaieties and pleasures of London, and the anxiety to return to her father at Loombe, were the result of the love for him, that she had thought was hopeless, and his affection for her redoubled in intensity as he poured out the ardour of his love and respect for the sweet girl at his side, and assured her that the devotion of his whole life should endeavour, in some slight measure, to atone for the suffering he had unwittingly caused her; that the knowledge of her love would give him fresh energy in his profession, and stimulate his exertions to increase his income sufficiently to enable him soon to take her to his heart, and give her a home worthy of her. He told her of his plans for the future; of all his hopes and ambitions; and she spoke to him of her dear old father, and acknowledged that, much as she loved Frank, she scarcely knew how she could bear to leave him, especially as he had been in failing health for the last year, and she sometimes thought the two Sunday services, and the constant visits he paid to the poor and sick in the parish, taxed his strength too severely.

"Do not be uneasy, darling," said Frank soothingly. "I also think perhaps the parish work here is at times too much for Dr. Grey; but we must wait awhile, and when I am able to offer my Ellen a comfortable home, rest assured we shall find a pleasant corner in it for your dear old father."

"Ah, Frank!" cried the girl, impulsively

throwing an arm round his neck, "how good you are! and how happy and proud I feel to possess your love."

Some natures are so delicately formed, that absorption of the life, of the very being is the result of a strong attachment. When Ellen believed that her love for Meredith was unresponded to, and tried so hard to overcome and conquer her feelings, it was to her like the withdrawal of sunshine and warmth from a flower, or the nourishment of the soil in which it grows, causing the blossoms to pale and the leaves to wither. A woman, when at last meeting the being for whom nature has allotted her, and feeling the affinity of mind and sentiments existing between them, gives her love truly unreservedly, and that love is her life.

Man *may*, and has, loved as intensely;

but, as a rule, *his* feelings are not so deeply engaged; expediency, change, absence, occupation, other interests and ties, may in time dissipate the impression, and disperse the dream of happiness he had once indulged.

The lovers sat long together, till the lengthening shadows across the pathway, and the deeper tints from the setting sun, that already shed a crimson glory on the rocky, rugged ascent to the Manor, warned Ellen that the day was waning, and indeed too late for her intended visit to Lady Leslie, if she wished to return home in time for her father's dinner. To keep him waiting and wonderingly uneasy at her absence, was impossible to the loving little daughter; so, hastily bidding her lover good-bye, and giving him permission to go in the evening to see her father, and spend an hour or two in her sweet society, Ellen tripped away, and Meredith, as he lingered yet awhile, seemingly loath to tear himself from the old tree that had afforded him rest, and the scene wherein he had first experienced the joy and rapture of his darling's love, raised a fervent prayer to Heaven that he might ever deserve the love of the sweet, innocent girl who had just left him, and might, by God's mercy, be enabled to make her happy and shield her from all sorrow and trouble, whilst his life passed peacefully and contentedly at her side.

CHAPTER IV.

THE JESUIT'S THREAT.

LADY LESLIE felt very anxious and frightened when she thought over her conversation with Meg, and remembered her statement, that Count Varani and the valet were on terms of intimacy. She had never thought of the latter as being in any way connected with her former lover, and the idea was revolting and horrible to her. She could not believe that Paolo would stoop to employ a spy in her husband's household, even to gain information of her, or admittance to her presence, and she thought, if there really *were* any acquaintance between them, it must be a casual one, and previously unknown to him, but the idea that Giuseppe had seen the Count, and knew perhaps that he had visited her, terrified her; she had refused to place herself in any communication with Paolo, so could not refer the matter to him, or ask how the valet had seen him, and how much he knew. She had promised to meet him on a certain day in the grounds of the Manor, and confide the boy to his care, but it yet wanted a week to the appointed time, and the thought that perhaps she was in the power of the Italian servant, and that he might betray her to Sir Charles, added greatly to the torture she endured. At last she determined to speak cautiously to the man, and to find out if possible how he knew Count Varani, and if he were aware of her having seen him that evening. Meg unceasingly begged her to confide all to Sir Charles, but she had promised Paolo to be silent, and she determined not to tell her husband until the boy had been safely transferred to his father's care, and until both had had time to leave the country. So the following day she sent for Giuseppe, and when he entered the boudoir, instantly accosted him, saying:

"Meg tells me there was an altercation last night, at the back garden gate, caused by some friend of yours leaving at a late hour, in a secret and suspicious manner; was it a relation from Italy?

If so, why not have asked permission for him to have supper with you openly? You know that I and Sir Charles are always kind to our servants' relations or old friends, and have no objection to their occasionally visiting them."

"Milady," said Giuseppe insolently, "I think *my* so-called *friend* was more *your* visitor that mine, since he passed some hours in your bed-room, and *I* only acknowledged he had been to see me to save him from being arrested by Mr. Morton!"

"Giuseppe," exclaimed Lady Leslie, still keeping command over herself, though her heart beat quickly, and she trembled from head to foot as she turned deadly pale. "What can you mean? How dare you say any man entered my room? Pray who admitted him then."

"I, milady," said the man; "I wouldn't keep two turtle doves longer apart."

"How dare you, fellow," said Leonora, haughtily, forgetting for a moment the strait in which she was placed through her indignation at the man's impertinence.

"I dare more than that, Lady Leslie, unless you think it worth your while to pay a heavy sum for my silence!"

"What mean you, sirrah? You forget yourself strangely," exclaimed Leonora, still endeavouring to show the valet that she did not fear him, though her visible trembling, and the ashen hue that overspread her countenance, belied the bold bearing she assumed.

"Oh no, Milady, *I* know well enough

what I'm about, and it's no use trying to brave it out with me. Sapristi! I can tell more of your past than you'd care to have confided to the servants and tenants on the estate!" Then lowering his voice he added more civilly, "But I've no intention to quarrel; pay me, and I'll serve you well and loyally, and arrange as many secret meetings with your lover as you wish, but defy me, and I may prove more dangerous than you wot of."

"I have no wish to defy you, or anyone," said Leonora faintly; "I have no idea what you know, or what induces you to threaten to injure a person who has never shown you aught but kindness. Can you tell me the man's name that left the garden last night?"

"Count Varani, Miladi, who fought a

duel on your account with Sir Charles Leslie, and who was your lover until your husband discovered your guilt; and who still loves you, and has followed you to England, in the hope of inducing you to fly with him."

"And which, as you know so much, I had better inform you, that I have no intention of doing," said the poor woman, with as much dignity as she could command. "Are you a minion of Count Varani? Is it possible that he can be so mean, so debased, as to employ a low spy in this house, and one who is capable of so grossly insulting me?"

"I am no low spy, Miladi," said Giuseppe angrily; "though my birth is not equal to that of Paolo Varani, I am bound to him by other ties, and to serve him, and advance the interests of my College, I consented for a time to hold this humble position."

"Jesuit College!" exclaimed Lady Leslie, more and more alarmed, "are you then sent by his foster brother, the Jesuit of Murano?"

"Yes, truly, for I am he!" said Giuseppe gravely.

Leonora, at last thoroughly cowed and terrified, hid her face in her hands, and burst into tears, whilst a sardonic grin passed over Giuseppe's stern features, as he looked at and seemed to gloat over her sorrow, but at last, he became impatient, and roughly said, "Weeping is useless! I don't wish to betray you. Give me your diamonds, and a bag of gold, and I will help you all in my power."

"Cane! Ladro!" cried Leonora, her temper now fairly roused, and disgust and indignation gaining possession, and overcoming for the moment the deadly fear that overwhelmed her. Then, as the natural pride and dignity inherent to her nature came to her aid, she motioned the valet to the door, saying, "Make me suffer as you will! I deserve it for ever having trusted you, or your foster brother; but the diamonds and the gold belong to my husband, and I will not rob him; though indeed, were they mine, not one precious gem, or piece of gold, would I give you. My life to me is little worth; the consumption that carried off my poor father, has seized hold of me also, and my days are numbered, but with my last breath I would say, 'I defy you!' Villain, leave my presence instantly, and never dare again to address me."

"Che furia! Che furia! Gently Miladi," said Giuseppe, seeing he had gone too far, and awakening to the fact that, if Leonora told Sir Charles of all that had passed between them, before he had been able to abstract the valuables, on the possession of which he had been so determined, that all his plans would be frustrated; he perceived the poor woman before him had more courage than he had given her credit for, and, mean scoundrel as he was, he could not help admiring her for it.

So he once more addressed her, and said, "Pay no more attention to my rough words! I love and esteem my foster brother too much ever really to injure a woman he has deigned to love. I will do nothing against you, and as soon as you have given him the child, according to your promise, we will both leave England, never to return."

" It is well," said Leonora, with a sigh of relief; "I gave my word not to tell Sir Charles, until Paolo, and my poor little boy, had had time to quit the country, so until then my lips are sealed, unless your threats and insolence had forced me to break my promise. Now leave me, I am ill and require rest."

When the man left her at last, poor Leonora's strength and courage gave way, and the agony was almost more than her enfeebled frame could well support. She sobbed bitterly, as she knelt, praying that the Virgin would look down on her grief, and teach her what course she ought to pursue. She longed to confide in her husband, and leave all trouble and responsibility with him, yet she shrank from doing so, dreading a repetition of the dreadful duel that had taken place at Venice. After a time, she bathed her eyes, tried to control her emotion, and appear calm and self-contained as usual, so that, when Meredith ran in hastily before dinner, and clasping her hand, exclaimed, " Dear Lady Leslie, I know you will congratulate me and be happy at my success; Ellen loves me!" Leonora was able to smile kindly at the young man, and tell him how glad she was that the dear girl they all so fondly loved, would have so good and loving a husband. Sir Charles, who had that day received a letter from Tony, written in better spirits, and a few lines from Lady Harman, saying the boy was rapidly getting over his sorrow and finding amusement and interest in the numerous picnics, water parties, *fetes champetres*, etc., that are always crowded into the last few weeks of the London Season, warmly shook the young barrister's hand, and wished him every possible happiness. And if he could not help regretting that his dear little godchild had not lent a favourable ear to his boy's suit, he felt that with Frank she would pass a tranquil, happy life, and that he could not wish a better fate for her.

CHAPTER V.

THE SHIPWRECK.

As Frank Meredith left the Manor, after dinner, to pay his promised visit at the Vicarage, he noticed a light dog-cart, with a strong powerful horse, standing half hidden by the large trees that overhung the drive. The horse was attached by the bridle to a tree, and impatiently pawed the ground evidently not understanding being thus tied up, and left alone. Frank paused for a moment, but thinking it must belong to some tradesman, or visitor to the servants' hall, and being anxious to lose no time in rejoining Ellen, he went on, and soon forgot the circumstance, without having noticed the tall figure that had crouched behind the cart, to avoid observation, on perceiving his approach. However, directly his footsteps died away in the distance, the man arose, and the moon shining on his face, disclosed the features of the Italian valet, Giuseppe. "Sapristi!" he exclaimed in Italian, "that lawyer fellow nearly caught me," then again leaving the trap, he ran eagerly to the house, leaped into the store-room window, that he had carefully unfastened half an hour previously, and from which he had already once before made his exit, having locked the door, to prevent any of the other domestics entering, to observe his movements.

The Butler, old Curtis, was out for the evening, having gone with his daughter to the Rectory, as it had been arranged that Meg was to sleep there that night, and be quietly married to Tom Morton the following morning. The valet had said nothing to the servants, at the Manor, of his meeting with Meg and our honest Tom; much to the astonishment of the latter, who on questioning the girl, and hearing that no remark had been made on the subject, shook his head, and declared the valet was a deep one, and *he* wouldn't care to trust him. Giuseppe had had a long conference with his brother that afternoon, after his interview with Leonora, and high words had passed between them, as Paolo refused to be longer led by the Jesuit, or even to confide his plans to him, so he had determined to take advantage of old Curtis and Meg's absence, to run off, carrying with him all he could lay his hands on. Having provided himself with skeleton keys, he noiselessly entered Lady Leslie's dressing-room, and whilst the family were at dinner abstracted the diamonds that, for generations, had belonged to the Squire's wife ; then he repaired to the store-room, and operated on a large iron safe, in which reposed the massive plate, that for years had been an heir-loom, from father to son, of the Leslies.

By slow degrees, and with much exertion, and journeying backwards and forwards, he carried all out to the dog-cart, in which he found a large chest, that he had purchased whilst in London, and had concealed in the shrubberies, for the purpose.

He packed all neatly in it, excepting the diamonds, which he carried in his breast pocket, and then, throwing a plaid loosely over it, he led the horse across the grass, so that the noise of hoofs and wheels should not be heard, until he reached a sufficient distance from the house, when, after avoiding the Lodge, he pressed horse and trap through the hedge, that he had that evening carefully levelled for the purpose, and through which he had previously admitted it. Once on the high road, he drove at a furious pace, till he arrived at a wood, not many miles from Berwick; here he halted to rest the horse, and see that all was right, for the chest, which at present was too heavy for him to move, had greatly tried the light springs of the dog-cart, not intended for so cumbrous a weight. On again he drove, not heeding the large drops of rain that began to fall, and the ominous look of the sky, that had all the evening presaged a storm. On he went, till the salt spray met his cheek, and he turned towards the sea, in a desolate, uninhabited part, about three miles from Berwick. Signs of life, however, were visible to-night, on the wild, gloomy shore, for a small Italian schooner was moored opposite, and a dingy pulled up on the beach, whilst two sailors lounged on the shingle, alternately gazing with dismay at the threatening clouds, and anxiously peering through the gathering gloom, for the approach of the cart, and their expected comrade.

"Eccomi alfin! Va bene?" exclaimed Giuseppe, as he threw the reins over the steaming horse's neck, and hastily jumped out. "Now lend a hand here, and off we go!"

"Ma Signore, guardate il nero ciel! Fa cattivo tempo!" * said the man doubtfully, whilst his companion positively refused to move, and when further urged, fell on his knees, saying Aves and Paternosters, and praying the Virgin to protect him.

"Get up, coward," said the Jesuit in Italian, "would you render my night's work of no avail? Do you not care to win the noble sum I promised each of you, if you landed me safely at a foreign port?

* " But, Signor, look at the black clouds. We shall have bad weather!"

Every instant's delay is dangerous; we may be pursued, and arrested. Better trust to the mercy of the elements, than to the hug of these Saxon bears. Besides," he added, looking round, I think it will turn to rain;" already heavy drops have fallen; let us get back to the schooner, and weigh anchor, before the wind rises." So saying he approached the cart, and the other men, after gloomily consulting together, made up their minds to risk it, and tried to move the chest, but it defied all efforts, and at last they determined to take out the contents by instalments, and make two or three journeys to the schooner.

Meanwhile the rain had ceased, and still the storm kept off, so Giuseppe persuaded the men that it was passing over, and cheered and stimulated them to fresh exertions, as they bent to their oars, and pulled lustily to the schooner. And now the last load was embarked, and the Jesuit unharnessed the mare, determining to leave her loose, but to hide the cart in a rocky cave that happened to be near.

All was at last completed to his satisfaction, and he accompanied the sailors in their last journey to the schooner, a small, low vessel, whose hull seemed utterly disproportioned to the tall masts it upheld, which, in their turn, supported a lighter set of spars, that tapered away until their upper extremities appeared no larger than the lazy pennant that vainly tried to display its length in the light breeze. The schooner had been built at Castellamare, originally for a wealthy merchant from

Naples as a pleasure yacht, then as her timbers became in parts rotten, the wily Neapolitan had her painted and patched up, and sold her cheap to a small trader, between Sicily and Naples, who brought coral and lava goods from the former island to the Neapolitan shopkeepers, who paid small sums for them, and sold them for three times their value to the rich English and American tourists who flock to Naples during the winter months. This trader had once been at the point of death, having caught malaria from being exposed to the night air on the marshes some miles from Venice, Giuseppe Varani had found him in a wretched hovel, without food or care, and had nursed and tended him, and thus saved his life, about a month before his brother's duel with Sir Charles Leslie.

A friendship thus sprung up between the two, and the Neapolitan trader, partly from gratitude, and partly from hope of the large reward promised to him and his men by the Jesuit if the expedition proved successful, had made the long journey to the Scotch coast, and had been laying about there for the last fortnight awaiting his orders.

Fair weather had favoured the little schooner in her journey from Naples; but the trader captain knew from experience that she was not too much to be trusted in a storm, and looked with anxiety at the threatening aspect of the sky and the heavy ground swell, that meant certain destruction if the gale that was brewing in the east came upon the small craft before she had escaped the too close vicinity of the rocks. As they rowed out further from the cliffs, the night was not so dark but objects could be discerned at some little distance, and in the eastern horizon a streak of fearful light impended over the gloomy waters in which the swelling outline formed by the rising waves became every minute more distinct and alarming. Dark clouds overhung the schooner as they embarked, and her tall masts apparently propped the black vapour, while a few stars were seen twinkling with a sickly flame in the streak of clear sky that skirted the ocean. Occasional light currents of air swept from the shore, but their flitting irregularity foretold them too surely to be the dying breath of the land breeze. The surf roared as it rolled to the beach, and made a dull monotonous sound, interrupted now and again by a hollow bellowing, as a bigger wave broke furiously against a cavity in the cliff. All, indeed, joined to render the aspect gloomy and portentous, as the captain and the four sailors under his command were earnestly engaged getting the schooner under way, whilst the Jesuit hastily replaced the silver in the chest and nailed it down securely.

"Ready the fore-royal!" cried the trader's shrill voice in Neapolitan, as he climbed far up a mast; "ready the fore-yard," uttered the hoarser tones of a sailor below. "All ready aft, Signor," cried a third man, and in a few minutes the order was given to "let fall." The falling sails now concealed the light which fell from the sky, and a deeper gloom was cast athwart the deck of the little vessel, giving to outward objects a still more appalling and dreary aspect.

The Jesuit, who had some slight knowledge of nautical matters, urged the sailors to speed, in getting clear of the land, muttering to the trader, "Remember we are on the enemy's coast, and I love it not well enough, to wish to lay my bones there." Gradually the sea was becoming more agitated, and the violence of the wind was steadily increasing. The latter no longer whistled amid the cordage of the vessel, but seemed to howl gloomily, as it passed through her spars and ropes. An endless succession of white surges rose above the heavy billows, and the very air was glittering with the light that was disengaged from the ocean. Still the little vessel kept on her course, tacking from side to side, and endeavouring to get further and further out to sea, as the first vivid flash of forked lightning, slowly followed by a heavy peal of thunder, warned them that the storm was approaching. The four Neapolitan sailors were almost paralysed by terror; the captain and the Jesuit only keeping cool, as the former shouted his orders through a short speaking trumpet he held in one hand, whilst he steadied himself with the other by grasping one of the shrouds of the vessel. But the sea became rougher and rougher, and in less than half-an-hour from the time the schooner lifted her anchor, she was driven along with tremendous fury by the full power of a gale of wind, that amounted to a hurricane. And now the flashes of lightning became more and more frequent, and the claps of thunder followed

instantaneously, seeming directly overhead.
The poor old vessel laboured hard against
the tempest, but the man at the helm cried
he was losing command, as she was no
longer obedient to her rudder; and as the
huge swelling waves heaved her alternately
high upon the surface and then plunged
her into the trough of the sea, a flash of
lightning revealed the awful fact that she
was driving in bodily towards the shore.
The Jesuit stood at the bow of the vessel,
frantically clutching the ropes to prevent
his being borne from the deck by the fury
of the waves as they dashed over it. " We
have no hope left us but to anchor," said
the captain. " Our ground tackle may yet
bring her up." The words were scarcely
out of his mouth, when a larger wave than
before broke over the doomed schooner,

whilst the next caused her to rise high in the air, only to settle heavily on the rocks, to which she had drifted. The shock was so violent as to throw all from their feet, and the universal quiver that pervaded the vessel was like the last shudder of animated nature. Another wave of great height followed almost directly, and, raising the vessel again, threw her roughly still further on the bed of rocks, and at the same time its crest broke over her quarter, sweeping the length of her decks with a resistless fury. The features of the Jesuit, as a vivid flash of lightning illuminated his swarthy countenance, expressed the malignant passion, greed, and baffled revenge, that formed the chief ingredients of his character. The chest containing the stolen plate lay at his feet, the diamonds were in his breast; the rich booty, to gain which he had served for weeks as a common menial, was at last his, but only to be snatched from his grasp, and become the prey of the ocean. The hollow noise beneath him, showed only too plainly that the water was breaking up the half-rotten timber of the poor old vessel. The Neapolitans knelt around him praying, save one, who, in terror, had cast himself into the seething waters, and had been instantly dashed to pieces against the rocks. The heavy groaning produced by the water in the timbers of the schooner, added its impulse to the raging feeling of the Jesuit, and, still clasping the jewels closer to his breast, he cast himself headlong into the sea, just as an overwhelming wave surmounted the wreck, and her timbers and planks gave way, and were swept towards the cliffs, bearing the bodies of the poor Neapolitan sailors among the ruins.

Giuseppe was a light and powerful swimmer, and the struggle was hard and protracted. The current swept him diagonally by the rocks, and he was forced into an eddy, where he continued to struggle, but with a force that was too much weakened to overcome the resistance he met. The next vivid flash of lightning showed the sinking form of the Jesuit, as it gradually settled in the ocean, still struggling, with regular but impotent strokes of the arms and feet, to gain the shore, and to preserve an existence that had been so much abused in its hour of allotted probation.

CHAPTER VI.

DISCOVERY OF THE ROBBERY.

It was late when old Curtis, the butler, returned home, after leaving Meg at the Vicarage, and he went straight to bed, so he did not discover the open window in the pantry, or suspect any mischief. He had arranged to be back at nine the next morning, as the wedding was to be a quiet and an early one, and the bride and bridegroom had decided to drive straight from the church to the station, and travel direct to Lancashire.

Meg, with her usual good sense, had

begged that it should be so settled, and no one but the immediate relations and dearest friends on either side had been invited, or indeed knew aught of the wedding, or even engagement.

Lady Leslie had given her faithful companion a complete trousseau, suitable to the change in her position, and would have been present at her wedding, had not the trying scene she had undergone with the Jesuit the day before completely prostrated her, leaving her neither strength or energy to rise at that early hour.

Sir Charles Leslie, Meredith, Ellen and Mr. Morton were present, also an uncle of Tom's on the mother's side, who had succeeded to the business of the grocer's shop in the small Lancashire town, and whose industry and energy had made so profitable an affair out of it, that he was now a comparatively rich man.

Curtis, and our old friend Maggie, the housekeeper (his wife), dressed in a neat dove-coloured silk, also a gift of Lady Leslie's for the occasion, and a young cousin of Meg's, holding a respectable position as an electrician, and already making a tidy income, completed the party, who now gathered round the altar to welcome our honest Meg, who, with Dr. Grey and Tom, entered from a side door, leading from the Vicarage.

Meg wore a soft cream-colored thin cashmere dress, with a little straw bonnet to match, and looked very sweet and pretty as she kissed her old parents, and shook hands with all present.

Miss Dora had made a terrible scene,

when told of Tom's intended marriage, and had positively insulted poor Meg, telling her she was a scheming impudent hussy, to dare to raise her eyes to her wealthy brother, but Meg's kind heart enabled her to make allowances for the ill-bred cotton lord's daughter, who had not yet recovered from the mortification she had endured, and her good sense stayed the retort that rose to her lips, and she answered with a modest dignity natural to her, "I deeply regret, Miss Morton, that you are displeased with your brother's choice, but I will not take offence; I hope some day you will think differently, and that we shall be united and happy together."

However, it seemed that poor Dolly's recent trials had not yet been sufficient to take down the false pride and stuck-up vanity that threatened to ruin her happiness for life; she positively refused to attend the wedding, or speak kindly to the bride, and Tom's anger and indignation at his sister's conduct would have caused a lasting breach between the brother and sister, had not Meg earnestly and unselfishly prayed her lover to moderate his wrath, and to leave Dora alone until she came to her senses. And now the old Vicar commenced the service, and soon Tom and his sweetheart had exchanged the solemn vows that united them for ever, and Dr. Grey pronounced them "man and wife." Then all the little party crowded to the Vestry, kissed and congratulated the bride, and wrung Tom Morton's honest hand, wishing him all happiness and prosperity.

Old Morton, who, although stuck-up and

purse-proud, had at the bottom a kind honest heart, implanted a ringing kiss on his pretty daughter-in-law's cheek, as he clasped a *rivière* of sparkling gems round her neck, and said, "God bless ye, my lass, be 'appy, and make my dear 'onest boy a loving wife. 'E deserves it, for 'e's allays been a good son to 'is old father, and though p'raps I say it, as shouldn't, you'll go a long way afore you find so good, upright, 'onest a man, as my Tom."

"May the Laird bless ye, and mak ye a kind gudeman to my ane bonny lassie," said old Maggie, as Tom kissed her, and told her that she and Mr. Curtis would ever be welcome and honoured guests at his Lancashire home. Tom had wanted the kind old couple to leave the Manor, and live near their daughter in Lancashire, but old

Maggie's faithful soul would not let her leave her dear Squire whilst she foresaw a sad trying time for him, for his wife seemed to be fading from their sight, and daily became thinner and weaker, and looked a shadow of her former self.

Kind old Maggie's feelings warmed towards the poor suffering woman, whose lined worn face and anxious eyes betrayed the disquiet of her spirit, and the faithful old creature longed to be able to help and comfort her, as her heart bled for the mistress whose silent misery was dragging her to an early grave, and whose patient uncomplaining manner, and invariable gentleness and kindness, endeared her to all around her. Meg, as she took leave of the Baronet, and thanked him for all his kindness, said, "Dear Sir Charles, my only sorrow on this happy day is caused by leaving dear Lady Leslie. I know you will always be kind and considerate to her; and tell her, that if ever she is in trouble or serious illness, that Meg will leave husband and home, and for a time neglect every other duty, to come to her and comfort her." Ah, Meg, as you drove off happily and contentedly with your dear Tom, and soon after left the little village station a happy loving wife, you little thought how soon you would be called upon to fulfil your promise, and how sad and painful would be your return to the home of your childhood!

But to-day, all must be peace and joy, and whatever distress the sorrows and troubles of others may eventually cause you, be thankful, Meg, that the good, honest-hearted fellow you so fondly love will help you to bear all trials, and the stout arm thrown so tenderly around you will henceforth shield and protect you, and his heart will ever be a haven of rest and consolation for you, amid the griefs and worrys that all have occasionally to suffer in this world of probation.

Sir Charles Leslie had been greatly astonished and displeased, when the young footman at the Manor had entered his room that morning to offer his services, saying that the valet, Giuseppe, was nowhere to be found, and that his bed had evidently not been slept in that night. The Squire, who was habitually kind and lenient to his domestics, could at times be very hard and severe, and he considered the Valet's conduct, in remaining out all night without permission, most impertinent and reprehensible, and he determined on his return to give him a stern reprimand. Curtis and Maggie having to leave so early to attend the wedding, had not gone into the room that especially belonged to them, in which, in a strong iron safe, the old Butler kept the family plate, and where Maggie had closets with piles of linen neatly arranged on shelves, each adorned by a few sticks of lavender and rosemary, and store cupboards containing rows of pots of jams and jellies, all carefully labelled, with other dainties and sweetmeats, that our Tony used to love, when, as a little rosy urchin, he climbed on to the cheery old Scotch woman's knee, whilst he eat the sweeties, and listened to the quaint Scotch ditties and innocent yarns that the old couple delighted in pouring into his youthful ears.

Tony, though absent, had not forgotten his former attendant and half playfellow, for Meg, as a girl of sixteen, when she accompanied the Leslies to Italy, was but a child herself, and used to enjoy a romp and game with the merry, roguish, little fellow, almost as much as he did.

So Tony sent her a wedding present, and wrote a kind, hearty letter of congratulation to Tom, that greatly pleased and gratified the young couple.

When Curtis returned to the Manor, with Sir Charles and Maggie, after the ceremony, he was instantly accosted by the footman, who, with a white scared face, and excited tones, enquired if he had visited the storeroom, before leaving in the morning.

"No! Why man, what is the matter?" said the Butler, alarmed, as he hastily followed the servant downstairs.

"Please, Sir, I found the window open, and marks of feet on the sill and on the ground outside; someone has evidently entered the room during the night. I remember perfectly fastening the window and putting up the shutter and large iron bar, but I found them in a corner of the room, and half hoped that you might have removed them, though I know it is always my business to do so."

Curtis rushed frantically to the iron safe, but the door yielded to his touch, before even he could insert the key, for it had only been pushed to, and the awful fact was speedily disclosed to the old butler and frightened footman that the safe was empty, and all the valuable plate that, from one generation to another, had so long descended to the Leslie family, had been stealthily abstracted.

The old man staggered under the weight of this calamity, and bitterly reproached himself for his neglect, in not entering the store-room the night before, to see that all was right previously to going to bed, whilst old Maggie threw her apron over her face, and cried openly, as she rocked herself to and fro in her trouble and despair.

"There's no help for it," at last exclaimed old Curtis, "I must go at once and tell Sir Charles. He is always kind and just, and won't blame us more than we deserve!"

So the poor old man, followed by his

wife and the terrified footman, tapped at the door of the Squire's study, where he was engaged opening the letters that had come by the early post.

"Come in!" called out Sir Charles, without turning from his desk. "Has Giuseppe returned?"

"No, Sir," replied Curtis sadly, as the tone of his voice, and a deep sob from Maggie, caused the Baronet to turn round quickly.

"Why, what's the matter?" he exclaimed, as he rose, and taking old Maggie's hand, forced her to sit down. "Come Mrs. Curtis, surely you have nothing to cry for on this bright morning, that you have seen your child so happily married!"

"Oh, Sir Charles!" began the butler, "that we should have lived to see this day, and have to tell you! I know I did wrong in not going into the store-room, sir, to see all was right when I returned last night."

"Why, man! Speak out! What is it?"

"The safe has been opened and the plate is stolen," blurted out old Curtis, as he leant against the wall for support.

For a minute a dead silence ensued, interrupted only by poor Maggie's sobs, as Sir Charles tried to collect his thoughts, and fully understand the blow dealt him by the Butler's words; at last, he held out his hand to the faithful old servant and said, "It is no fault of yours, Curtis! Don't cry Mrs. Curtis, dear Maggie! Cheer up! All may not be gone; now I'll come down and investigate, and then we must take immediate steps to recover it!"

So saying, Sir Charles led the way to the store-room, the footman assuring him that he had carefully fastened and barred the window, as usual, but had found it open this morning.

The Squire examined the shutters and bar, and soon declared that they had not been forced from the outside; then he looked attentively at the marks on the window-sill, and the footprints on the mould beneath the window, which he tracked some little distance till they became lost in the grass, where, however, the marks of wheels were distinctly visible.

"And Giuseppe absent," said the Baronet, as a dark suspicion entered his mind, and he determined to question all the other servants as to when the valet was last seen among them. But before all could be ascertained, a messenger arrived from the village inn, asking what accident had happened, stating that the valet had last night hired a horse and trap, saying it was for a friend of the Squire, and that the mare had just found her way back to the stable in a sorry plight, having evidently been out all night in the storm.

Suspicion then strongly pointed to Giuseppe, and Sir Charles instantly determined that a search for him must at once be instituted. He despatched Curtis to give notice at the small police-station at Loombe, and to make all possible inquiries in the village, whilst he ordered his horse to ride to Berwick and see what information he could gain there, before he telegraphed to Scotland Yard for a detective to be sent immediately from London.

Before leaving, Sir Charles entered Lady Leslie's room and told her he had to go to Berwick on important business, but would be back in time for dinner. He said nothing to her of the robbery, fearing it might agitate her, and gave strict injunctions to the servants not to alarm her by mentioning that, or even Giuseppe's absence.

The Squire carefully traced the wheel-marks on the grass till they brought him to the gap in the hedge, where Giuseppe had levelled it, and through which, the evening before, he had pressed the mare and dog-cart. He now felt no doubt of the valet's guilt, and once on the high road, gave the spur to his horse and galloped furiously till he reached Berwick, and alighted at our old friend Mr. Smith's office.

He soon explained his errand, and John

Smith accompanied him to the police-station, where he preferred the charge against the Italian valet, of stealing the family plate. The loss of the diamonds had not been discovered when he left. The Police Inspector and most of his men were absent, having been called off to the sea-shore by a fisherman, who reported he had that morning found several dead bodies, besides spars and masts of a ship, that had evidently been wrecked during last night's storm, a few miles off Berwick on the sea-coast.

Sir Charles, after telegraphing to Scotland Yard for a detective, and making fruitless inquiries about the valet in the town, joined the crowd of people that were flocking to the beach to see the remains of the wreck, fearing they might recognise some friend or relation in the dead bodies that had been washed ashore.

The day was delightful, as the Baronet started for his walk to the sea, anxious to look out upon the state of the ocean, agitated as it must still be by the tempest of the day before. Little fleecy clouds were now scattered on the horizon, with just enough motion in the air to float them occasionally over the sun, and so chequer the landscape with that variety of light and shade, which often gives to a bare and unenclosed scene, for the time at least, a species of charm only found in a cultivated and planted country. Sir Charles soon arrived on the verge of the cliff, composed of the soft and crumbling stone called sand-flag, which gradually becomes decomposed, and yields to the action of the atmosphere, and is split into large masses, that hang loose upon the edges of precipices until, detached from them by the violence of the tempest, they descend with great fury into the vexed abyss below. Numbers of these huge fragments now lay strewed beneath the cliff from which they had fallen, whilst the tide foamed and raged amongst them. The wide sea still heaved and swelled with the agitation of yesterday's storm, which had been far too violent in its effects on the ocean, to subside speedily. The tide therefore poured on the beach with a fury deafening to the ear, and dizzying to the eye, threatening instant destruction to all at the time involved in its current.

The sight of nature, in her magnificence, or in her beauty, or in her terrors, has at all seasons an overpowering interest, and

Sir Charles paused to look out upon that unbounded war of waters, which rolled in their wrath majestically beneath him.

But he saw the crowd collected on the beach, and quickly determined to join them, and discover if possible what ship had been the victim of last night's storm, so he turned to a cleft in the precipice containing a rugged path, which was a short cut to the shore, though a somewhat dangerous one, as often large masses of earth, to which he was about to entrust his weight, gave way before him, and thundered down into the tormented ocean, and occasionally a detached fragment rushed after him, as if to bear him headlong in its course.

But the Squire had a courageous heart, a steady eye and a firm foot, so in a few minutes he joined the little crowd on a small projecting spot of stones, sand, and gravel, that extended a little way into the sea, which on the right hand lashed the very bottom of the precipice, and on the left, was scarce divided from it by a small wave-worn portion of beach, that reached as far as the foot of the cleft in the rocks by which he had descended.

Last night, when the schooner split to pieces, all at first seemed to be swallowed up in the ocean, then gradually floated upon the waves, excepting only a few pieces of wreck, casks, chests and such like, which a strong eddy, formed by the reflux of the waves, had landed, or at least grounded, upon the shallow where Sir Charles now stood. Amongst these, though dragged higher up on the beach by the humanity of the town folks, lay four corpses, closely guarded by a policeman. The faces of three of them were so battered by being dashed against the rocks as to be unrecognisable, but their clothes, and the swarthy colour of their skin, showed them to be of southern origin. The fourth man, however, had evidently been a strong swimmer, and thus protected himself in some degree, for though his features were livid and disfigured, they were otherwise unhurt. His apparel was of a finer texture and different form to that of his companions, and his short light tweed jacket was buttoned tightly across the breast, eliciting the remark from the seafaring crowd, that those foreigners had queer ways with them, not to doff jacket and give the arms more power, as our British tars would have done.

Sir Charles Leslie shuddered at the sight of the dead bodies, and would have passed without a closer inspection, had not something in the form of the last corpse arrested his attention; and on approaching it, an exclamation of horror rose to his lips, as he beheld the well-known face of his late valet, Giuseppe. Just at that moment, a cry of astonishment and interest resounded from the mob assembled, as a still larger chest than those already found, was washed ashore.

The Baronet, turning, little thought the chest contained the silver he had lost, restored by the ocean; but, advancing, he gave his card to the Police Inspector, identified one of the corpses, as belonging to his late valet, and told of the robbery that had taken place at the Manor, and that he strongly suspected the Italian had been the thief. On closely examining the man's corpse, the policeman opened the jacket, so tightly buttoned across his chest, and found, concealed in the breast-pocket, a splendid *rivière*, coronet, bracelets, and five large stars, of diamonds of the purest water, which Sir Charles instantly recognised as the family jewels, that had belonged to his mother and grandmother, and with which he had felt such pleasure in adorning his beautiful Italian bride, on the day of his wedding.

Not being aware of the loss of the diamonds, before leaving the Manor, and fearful lest his wife, in her weak state, should discover the robbery and be alarmed during his absence, Sir Charles hurried away, having promised to attend the inquest on the following day; and, charging the police to have the sea-shore well-searched and guarded, lest more of his property should be disgorged by the ocean, whilst he confided the diamonds already found to their care.

CHAPTER VII.

SIR CHARLES LESLIE STOOD BEFORE THEM.

WHEN the Squire had left, for his ride to Berwick, Leonora feebly and languidly rose, and was just dressed when Ellen Grey arrived; and, after many inquiries for her health, and regrets at seeing her so weak and ill, she threw her arms round her neck, and told her of all her new-found happiness—as she at last acknowledged, the grief, Frank Meredith's previous coldness had caused her. The young girl, already, looked a different being; love and joy gave depth and brilliancy to the lustre of her dark blue eyes; elasticity returned to her step; the arch playfulness of her demeanour and merry prattle again delighted all around her, whilst the affection she bore to Leonora, and the sorrow and anxiety caused by her illness, added a soft tenderness to her manner, which increased its charm.

Poor Lady Leslie, whose mental and bodily sufferings, at this moment, were very great, was cheered and comforted by her young friend's presence; and when, after lunch, Ellen left her, accompanied by Frank, on her return to the Vicarage, Leonora felt slightly strengthened, and thought she would take a little stroll in the grounds of the Manor, whilst she awaited Sir Charles' return.

In the western portion of the gardens,

that looked over the Vicarage, and the most ancient part of the village of Loombe, stood some old ruins, half covered with ivy, and around which large old trees had found root, mantling the ruinous walls with their dusky verdure. There, could be obtained a complete and commanding view of the decayed part of the village, that had been originally constructed in the humble style of the Scotch cottages built a hundred years ago, and the most part of which had long been deserted—as testified by their fallen roofs and blackened gables. On a few of these hovels the rafters, varnished with soot, were still standing, like skeletons, and some others, partially covered with thatch, appeared still tenanted, for the peat fire smoke crept upwards, not only from the chimneys, but from various other crevices in the roof, as the inhabitants prepared their humble meals. As years rolled on, Nature, always changing, but renewing as she changes, had supplied, by the power of vegetation, the fallen and decayed signs of human labour. The small gardens had once been surrounded by little pollards, that had now grown into large, tall, forest trees ; the branches of the fruit-trees had extended over the verges of the little yards, whilst quantities of dock, nettles and hemlock concealed the ruined walls, and converted the whole scene of desolation into a picturesque bank of a forest. Leonora looked down mournfully on the above view as, after sitting an hour on the upper terrace, and resting every five minutes as she wandered down the slope, she at length arrived at the moss-covered ruins of a low wall, that afforded her a pleasant resting-place. Her light footstep scarcely sounded on the grass-grown path, and was inaudible to Meredith, who, after leaving Ellen at the Vicarage, had climbed from this wall on to a little ledge beneath, to gather some ferns and wild flowers, whose luxuriant beauty had attracted him, and that he fancied Ellen might like. Scarcely, however, was Lady Leslie seated, than Paolo Varani, whose footsteps were, by some evil genius, impelled to the spot, drew aside the bracken and copse-wood, that half concealed an arch-way that had formerly led to a tower, and, springing towards her, threw himself at her feet, clasping her hands, and kissing them with love and fervour.

But Leonora quickly moved from him, and rising with dignity, said, " No Paolo, do not touch me! Your brother has told me of the base plan you concocted between you! You knew that he was living in my husband's house as a common menial, that he might act as spy over my movements. Yesterday he threatened me with exposure, and endeavoured to extort gold and jewels from me, to insure his silence, but I told him to do his worst; I would not rob my husband. The gold, the diamonds are his, and are not mine to give, but did I possess all the wealth of Arabia, the treasures of India, not one baioccho would I give him! And now, Paolo, I implore you to leave England at once. The shock and horror that your brother has caused me, are not easy to forgive, and the thought that you approve his conduct, and are perhaps ready to act as he has done, has given me so painful an impression, and caused me so terribly to mistrust you, that forgive me, but I cannot, I dare not, confide my darling child to your care. I could not die in peace, thinking that he would be taught the deceit and dishonesty of your wicked foster brother."

"Leonora," exclaimed Paolo, "would you then break your word to me? Would you drive me to despair? Surely you cannot imagine that *I* approve Giuseppe's insulting you, as he did yesterday!"

"You knew that he was concealed in the house, and through him *you* gained admittance. I was not safe from your

persecution, even in my own bed-chamber, and now, your persisting in following me, and in determining to see me against my will, have caused my illness, and my death will soon follow. All I beg of you is to leave me. Be content, let me die in peace."
As Leonora uttered the last words, a faintness came over her, and she staggered and leant against the wall for support. At the sight of her suffering, Paolo's tenderness for her returned, and, again, on his knees, he implored her to forgive him. The poor woman tried hard to command herself, and overcome the deadly faintness that overpowered her senses; notwithstanding all his faults, she still loved Varani; she felt that she could not respect him, but he was the lover of her youth, the only being that

had won her heart, and she must dismiss him for ever. She must say a last eternal adieu to him, never again to meet in this world. For a moment the cold reserve, so unnatural to her, that she had forced herself to show, gave way, and the woman's loving faithful heart gained the ascendancy as she bent over Paolo, and his arms once more stole around her, as he kissed her passionately, and renewed his prayers and entreaties to her to fly with him.

"No, dear," she answered, "it is impossible; I am a dying woman; my duty is to my husband, to my children. I will not disgrace them, and leave them to scorn and condemn me after my death. I sinned once, and with my life I hope this sin may be expiated. When I pray, I seem to feel the Holy Virgin looks down kindly and compassionately on me, and intercedes for me at the Throne of Grace. Good-bye, dear Paolo! I do not ask you to forget me; our affection was too deep for that, and was part of our lives; but try, dear, to be a better, a holier man! Turn for comfort and strength to Him who alone can give it, and who died to save us, poor weak sinners, and let us both hope that, in another and brighter world, free from the trammels of earth and wickedness, our souls may meet, in pure and peaceful communion, where no sin or wicked passions can enter to disturb our lasting happiness." So saying, Leonora throws her arms for the last time round her lover's neck, and with one long kiss is about to bid him an eternal farewell, when a hasty footstep is heard, and Sir Charles Leslie stood before them.

He started back with horror and amazement on perceiving the man he had thought dead, and exclaimed in anguish, "Varani alive, and again with my wife."

Leonora with a low moan hid her face in her hands, whilst Paolo's impetuous temper, excited by the (to him) hateful presence of the man who had stolen the joy and happiness of his life, broke forth in a torrent of abuse and imprecation.

"Yes," he shouted, "I *am* alive and ready to fight you again, when you will! Yea, I would fight you with redoubled energy. Would not the sight of my darling's sufferings lend courage to my heart and strength to my arm? Brute! Devil that you are! You are killing her!

You have taken all joy from her existence! Don't you see that her strength is failing, her life slowly ebbing away, in your accursed country, and through your hateful presence! She is pining for the only one she ever loved! You can only keep her from me yet awhile, till she dies, and then you will be her murderer."

"Hush, Paolo," said Leonora faintly. "Go, I pray you, instantly," then turning to her husband, she said, in despairing accents, "Charles! Do not blame me now, for indeed, indeed, I do not deserve it."

The Squire looked sorrowfully at her, but would say nothing in Varani's presence. He coldly and courteously entreated her to return to the house, and as she obeyed him, and, with feeble, tottering steps, dragged herself slowly away, he turned once more to Varani, and said in bitter accents—" You accuse *me* of killing her! What then has been *your* conduct ? You first ruined, and have now pursued this unhappy woman, who had the misfortune to love you; you deprived her of peace, and innocence, and of her husband's affection. Instead of determining never again to see her, when you found she still cared for you after her marriage, you fanned the flame of her unworthy passion, till she forgot honour, husband, and child; and for your sake, and at your entreaty, sacrificed her pride and self-respect, and all a woman should hold dear. Now you again persecute her, and endeavour still to ruin her life, and make her name a by-word and a scorn!

No, whilst I have the power, whilst life still animates my body, I will defend her from you! Go! Leave my sight for ever! Dare not again to approach Lady Leslie, for I tell you, and give you fair warning, that if I again find you lurking on my estate, you shall be arrested as a poacher and intruder, and, at the hands of Justice, shall meet the only fate you merit. I will never again fight you. Duels are for honourable men, not for such scum of the earth as you have proved yourself."

Varani, though livid with rage, quailed before the Baronet's proud and defiant gaze, and after shaking his fist at him, and muttering a vow of vengeance between his teeth, turned, and hastily left his presence. Sir Charles, when alone, paused, as the memory of the past and all he had suffered arose vividly before him. The great tide of life ebbed and flowed in his heart as in the ocean. The stormy waves that had urged him on in youth to the rocks and shoals of active life, had receded back upon the quiet depths, and left the strand bare. Pride had helped to console him in grief, and had supported him against fraud and deceit, as a champion and a fortress. This pride did not arise from a knowledge of his integrity and mental gifts, still less did it spring from the vulgar common places of birth and fortune; it rather resulted from a wholesale and supreme contempt of other men, their objects and ambitions, and of the stern business of life. He had been proud of his struggles against the sins and temptations of the world, and prouder still of conquests over his own passions; but now, as he reflected on the misery that had resulted from his marriage to the wife he had so dearly loved ; as he thought of the eighteen years of sadness, a youth consumed in silent sorrow over the grave of Joy, and how powerless he had been to alleviate her sufferings, his courage gave way, and he hid his face in mute, but intense agony.

If Leonora should really die of a broken heart; if her grief had been more than she could bear; if he had strained justice into cruelty, and without pity, for the victim of a mother's treachery, could he ever forgive himself? Then the remembrance of Leonora's last deceit to him returned; of the fervent embrace he had just beheld between her and Varani; and again his heart was steeled against her, and he determined never to pardon this fresh dereliction from the path of duty.

CHAPTER VIII.

SICK UNTO DEATH.

WHEN Lady Leslie returned to the Manor, she remained for some time weeping miserably, the heavy sobs seeming to shatter and rend her now weak frame. Poor woman! Her cup of sorrow was indeed full, and she could only welcome and look forward to death to release her from her sufferings.

She seemed turned to stone as Sir Charles entered her room, and said, in stern cold accents:—

"Leonora, you have again deceived me! I grieve for you, ill and unhappy as you are, but you must leave my house. I cannot forgive you a second time."

"Charles," said his wife, solemnly, "do with me as you will, but I am not again guilty, and do not deserve your anger."

"Not deserve it, Madam, when I found you in your lover's arms!"

"Had you heard all that passed between us, you would exonerate me from further evil. I did not willingly meet Paolo Varani; he came upon me unexpectedly. I first knew that he was alive the night of Mr. Morton's ball, though I did not then speak to him, for his sudden appearance so greatly terrified me, that I fainted, as you know. Since then he has several times forced himself into my presence, but I have always begged and implored him to leave me, and even now, when you discovered us together, I was bidding him farewell for ever."

"A likely story," said the Squire bitterly, as he remembered the passionate kisses he had silently witnessed. "No, Leonora, I cannot believe you! I have tried hard to gain your love, but at last I am convinced it is hopeless. You cannot even feel common respect for me, or you would not, close to my house, and notwithstanding my kindness and forbearance towards you, allow your paramour to embrace you and linger at your side."

"Charles, I confessed to you long ago that I had loved Paolo since my childhood; you know how my poor mother deceived us all. Could you expect me coldly to say good-bye for ever to the lover of my youth? I know I *was* wrong even to let him approach me; but have *some* pity on me! Indeed, indeed, I have been sorely tried! but beyond the farewell kiss you saw, I have not again failed in my duty towards you."

"Enough!" said the Baronet, "pray say no more. Now that Count Varani is alive, and you evidently still love him, some trouble is sure to follow. As far as lies in my power, I will still protect you and save you from disgrace; but as soon as I can arrange it, you must quit my roof, and I can only try to banish you from my heart as I must from my home."

So saying, the Squire turned and slowly left the room.

All that night faithful old Maggie watched at her poor mistress' bedside, not caring to leave her to a comparative stranger, and the next morning, when Dr. Quin arrived as usual, he found his patient so much worse, that he thought it necessary to warn Sir Charles that the fatal disease was making such quick progress that he feared his wife's days were numbered, and that it baffled his skill, as no medicine could arrest it. The Baronet was sorely perplexed, and knew not what to do. Yesterday's scene had convinced him that Leonora was again faithless to him, and he had determined to part from her for ever. His whole soul revolted at this (as he thought) repetition of infidelity, and the deceit that had been practised upon him.

He felt that as Paolo Varani was alive, it was useless for him to endeavour, or hope, ever to win his wife's affection, and he became reluctantly convinced that the old love of her youth was too deep and strong to be eradicated. He had intended still to act kindly and honourably to her, and indeed his heart bled for her suffering, though he severely blamed her for again (as he imagined) giving way to an illicit passion. He had determined to make her a handsome allowance, and to send her and her little boy back to her mother at Venice, feeling that this course was best for her happiness, and would save him and his son from the disgrace that the discovery of her guilt would surely, sooner or later, bring on them. But now, when Dr. Quin gravely told him of Lady Leslie's serious condition, and held out little or no hope of her recovery, adding that he feared something was on her mind, and that she ought to be kept calm and peaceful, and if possible happy, the Squire felt it would be cruel to pursue the course he had intended, and that common humanity demanded that he should see Leonora and endeavour to soothe her by the assurance of his pity and forgiveness. So he entered her room, and found her lying on a sofa, drawn near the window, sadly gazing at the landscape, whilst old Maggie tenderly bent over her, trying to persuade her to swallow the medicine just sent. On seeing her husband the poor woman nervously started and imploringly held out her hand.

Sir Charles took it, and patted it kindly, as he begged her not to distress herself about anything he had said, and assured her that he would do nothing hastily or unkindly. But Leonora could not be satisfied with this, and unceasingly asserted her innocence of the fresh sin that had been imputed to her. Sir Charles could not believe her; but seeing how weak and ill she was, and remembering the doctor's strict injunctions, he only answered soothingly, and implored her not to worry about anything, but only try to get well and regain a little strength.

Frank Meredith, as our readers will doubtless remember, had climbed to a small ledge, directly beneath the place of the unfortunate meeting between Varani and Leonora, that had been so suddenly interrupted by the Baronet, and being unable to leave it without observation, had been a secret and unwilling listener to all that passed. The young barrister was deeply attached both to Sir Charles, and Lady Leslie, and was terribly pained at the dark mystery he had unwittingly discovered. He had always suspected and feared that Leonora was not happy, and he felt there was some tangled skein in her past life, that it were best and kindest not to attempt to unravel, but he had no idea of the truth, thus suddenly revealed to him, and when he thought of all her kindness and gentleness, and how his dear Ellen loved and respected her, he felt the strongest sympathy and pity for her sorrow, and his manly, honest nature made him long intensely to succour and support one so tried, and weak, and suffering. He debated long with himself, as to the right course to pursue. Should he tell Sir Charles all he had overheard, and exonerate his wife from further blame, by describing how firmly she had refused all Varani's offers and entreaties? Would not the Squire blame him for interfering, and feel annoyed that even *he* should know anything of the past? Meredith could not make up his mind what he ought to do, and at last decided to wait a few days, and see what line of conduct the Squire had determined on, and then, if it were in his power, to assist and defend the poor woman he so deeply pitied, no personal consideration, or fear of offending, should prevent his intercession. He said nothing to Ellen on the subject when he paid his usual evening visit to the Rectory, and he only hoped that the young girl's pure, innocent mind, might never be shocked by the sad tale of sin and misery, that had darkened the existence of one so dear to her.

But Leonora's illness soon showed that no human kindness, or cruelty, would long have the power to affect her; the signs of approaching death were already visible in her face; and though her husband evidently did not believe in her immediate danger, and buoyed himself with the hope that this, like former attacks, would pass over, all others around her were convinced that the end was near.

Dr. Quin called two days later, to consult the Vicar about sending for Tony, who had just started for Switzerland with his aunt, Lady Harman, whilst he telegraphed to London to request the attendance of an eminent physician, for consultation; not that the good old country doctor believed any skill could assist his patient, but as a satisfaction to himself, and her friends afterwards, to know that all that was possible had been done to save her.

Dr. Grey took the responsibility on himself of sending off a telegram to Tony, informing him of his poor mother's dangerous state, and begging him to return immediately, whilst another was despatched to Venice, conveying the sad news to Leonora's mother, and advising her to journey to England without delay, if she wished to see her daughter again in this world.

At Lady Leslie's express request, a letter had also been despatched to an old Roman Catholic priest, at Berwick, who had often visited her, and said mass in the Oratory, and to whom she had been in the habit of confessing, begging him to come to her without delay. Ellen Grey was sadly distressed, and spent most of her time at the

Manor, doing all in her power to cheer and comfort the friend who had been so kind to her, and relieving old Maggie's watch by spending hours by her bedside or sofa, to which she was assisted for a few hours every day.

Meg Morton had written cheerful, loving letters, both to her old parents and to Lady Leslie, describing her happy Lancashire home, but Leonora had especially forbidden any one to tell her of the sudden increase of her illness, not wishing to distress the faithful, kind-hearted girl, and throw a shadow over the first few days of her married life.

So Ellen and the old housekeeper, divided the charge of nursing the poor woman between them, assisted by the new maid, who, although willing and anxious to help, was comparatively useless, as the sufferer could not bear to see a stranger about her, and seemed so to cling to Ellen, and old Maggie, that one or the other never left her. Kind old Dr. Grey was often at the Manor, doing and saying all he could think of to comfort his old friend, Sir Charles, and often spending hours by his wife's couch, reading to her and helping the Catholic Priest to soothe her last days by the comfort of holy words and thoughts, and lead her to trust in God alone and look forward to eternal joy and peace in a happier and better world. For both men were true Christians, and the difference of Creed and religious opinions were forgotten in the presence of the Arch Destroyer, and their only aim was to lessen suffering, and smoothe the path to Eternity.

And so passed several days, without any perceptible change in Leonora, though she gradually became weaker, and the London Physician, that had attended Dr. Quin's summons, shook his head, and gravely confessed he was powerless to combat the disease that had taken so firm a hold of his patient. A telegram from Tony announced his immediate return, and he was expected daily. Also Leonora's mother, the old Marchesa Marchetta, telegraphed she would leave Venice immediately, and hoped to arrive at Loombe in a few days.

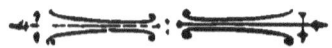

CHAPTER IX.

VARANI AND HIS SON.

The little Luigi had taken a great dislike to Kitty, Lady Leslie's new companion, and lost no opportunity of irritating and annoying the girl, who, not being so good-tempered as our Meg, was inclined to punish the young master, for his impertinence, and worry him in return. Now it happened one afternoon, a few days after the events recorded in our last chapter, that Kitty was sent to the village, to fetch some medicine for her mistress, and had been told to take the boy with her, to give him exercise. There had been heavy rain the night before, and mud and water lay on the pathway, large puddles making it in some parts almost impassable. The boy persisted in jumping into these pools, splashing up the mud into Kitty's face, and over her dress, and making himself in a terrible plight. The trick, commenced thoughtlessly, was continued, when the child saw the trouble and annoyance it caused the girl, who remonstrated with him at first kindly, then angrily, telling him she would give him a good whipping, if he were so naughty. High words arose between them, till Kitty, completely losing her temper, seized her little tormentor and shook him, saying she would not let him go till he promised to be good. A stormy scene ensued, when, at last, the boy eluded her grasp, and ran at full speed towards the shrubbery, where the thick bushes quickly concealed him from view.

Kitty, frightened at the child's sudden disappearance, screamed after him to return, and hastily started in pursuit, tearing her gown with the brambles, and inwardly vowing, that she would sooner leave her comfortable place, and good wages, at the Manor, than have the charge of such a mischievous, irritating, little Imp. The boy, in a fury, rushed heedlessly along, till his foot caught in a loose branch that lay across the path, and he fell his full length on the ground. Before he could rise, an arm was gently thrown round him, and he was raised tenderly by a tall, dark man, whose appearance seemed to exert some subtle influence over the child, who smothered the angry words that rose to his lips, and stared, open-mouthed and amazed, at the stranger.

"*Adorato mio bambino*," said the man, still keeping his arm around the boy, and addressing him in Italian. "At last I can touch you, can hold you in my arms."

"And who are you that care to hold me in your arms?" retorted Luigi. "No one here loves me, but my mother, and she is ill, and I listened and overheard them say she would die."

"And do you love your mother, Luigi?"

"*Si, si*," said the boy. "I love no one else here though, now Giuseppe's gone. He was right, when he called them a pack of English bears, and dogs of heretics. Ah! when will Giuseppe come back?"

"I know not," said the man, who doubtless my readers have already recognised as Count Varani, then seizing the advantage the child's liking for the Jesuit gave him, he added quickly: "Will you come with me and try to find him?"

The boy hesitated, but at last said: "No, I won't leave mama."

"But if she dies, and leaves you alone with these brutes? Would you be happy with them? You tell me no one loves you; why not come with me to our beautiful Italy, and be loved and petted, as if you were my own child?"

"But why do you want to take me?" said Luigi, suspiciously. "I would like to get away from Kitty, and what a row she would get into, if she had to go home and say she had lost me," he added with a grin.

"I want you because I love you, darling,

and wish to make you happy," said Varani, again drawing his child to his heart, and stooping to kiss him.

"But who are you, and why do you care for me?" persisted the boy.

"Will Luigi keep a secret, and not even tell his mother?" said Paolo, looking searchingly at the child.

"Oh! I never tell, if I think there's anything to gain by keeping quiet."

"Well, then, I am a relation," said Varani, "and want to take you away, where no Kitty shall teaze my darling, to a land where no fogs and damp will hurt you, and a bright sun and clear sky shall cheer and comfort you, and give you fresh life and joy. Will you come?"

"I'll think about it," said the boy, with a gravity beyond his years.

"What! can you hesitate?" said his father. "Come now! At once!"

"Nay, nay," said Luigi, "but I'll meet you in two days, and will not tell anyone. I s'pect I'll come. Hark!" he whispered, "there's Kitty coming after me. I'll cut down this way and give her the slip. She richly deserves to be frightened, and I hope they'll scold her well at home. An impudent, low hussy, to dare to speak to *me*, as she did. I'll punish her, for her insolence to me, a Baronet's son." So saying off struts the little urchin, with his head high, and his small figure drawn up to its full height, with a large idea of his own importance. Varani, left alone, thought over all the boy had said, and the knowledge that Leonora was so ill, caused him many a bitter pang. With all his faults his heart was faithful, and his intense affection for the poor woman who had suffered so bitterly, through her love for him and her mother's wicked deceit, made him half mad at the fear of losing her for ever. That night, when all was quiet at the Manor, Varani might have been seen pacing up and down, and praying beneath her window, till dawn, and the rural sounds that followed, warned him he must shun observation.

How could he see her again? How beg her forgiveness for the last trouble he had brought on her? How persuade her still to trust her darling boy to his care? The child had promised to meet him in two days' time; till then, he must wait even for tidings of Leonora, unless indeed she went out, and he was able again to waylay her.

He little knew how much worse she was, since the day he had seen her, or how impossible it was, now, for her even to walk that short distance.

CHAPTER X.

THE HONOURABLE GEORGE.

Miss Dora Morton, having partially recovered from the shame and annoyance Lord Booby's conduct had caused her, and being determined to show him that notwithstanding the disappointment she had suffered she could easily find a titled suitor willing and anxious to fall a victim to her charms, persuaded her father to give a grand dinner party, inviting all the County families, and as many grandees from London as might be induced, by the heat of the Dog-days in town, to escape for a short time from the steamy, heavy atmosphere of the Metropolis, and enjoy the fresh northern air, and excellent cuisine, always to be found, at the cotton spinner's residence. It happened that, in the early days of Lord Booby's courtship to the fair Dora, he had introduced a brother officer of his, a young lieutenant in the Horse Guards, who, although he had unmercifully quizzed Booby on the plebeian alliance he contemplated, had been only too glad to accept invitations to Belgrave Square, and to avail himself of the good dinners, suppers, and luncheons, therein provided.

The Morton's (both father and daughter) had made a great fuss over this young fellow, because he was an Earl's son, and belonged to a good old Irish family, who, though decayed and impecunious, still held an excellent position in Society.

The Honourable George Mullingar was a very young, short, dark-haired individual, who had not long left the nursery, and who, notwithstanding his Eton education, accepted old Morton's invitation, in a letter, written in a schoolboy's handwriting, with occasional faults of spelling and caligraphy. But, if he had not greatly profited by his school labour, he had mastered a lot of other accomplishments, marvellous for one of his size and age. He is a famous horseman, and one of the best shots in England. He is well-known on the Turf, and nobody was ever "too much" for him, either in the stable or the gambling room. His father can only make him a small allowance, but, with the help of post-obits and Jewish friends, he contrives to live in a splendour befitting his rank. He smokes and drinks as much as any two of the biggest men in his distinguished regiment. He rode his horse Spitfire, and won the famous Grand National Steeplechase, and, under friends' names, has horses entered at half the races in England, for his father, the old Earl, is a strict hand, and would never forgive him for gambling or betting.

With such grand accomplishments, who can say how far he may rise? He may take to politics, in his old age, and be a Prime Minister after Mr. Gladstone's own heart! Under his auspices, even the " dead bill " may be brought to life.

But he had lost heavily at the last Newmarket races, and was just now at his wits' end to know how to meet all the bills out against him, and to prevent their coming to the knowledge of his august sire. So he hailed old Morton's invitation with delight, as he thought, at least, in the remote village of Loombe, he would be safe for a time from his creditors, and if he could but lie "perdu" there for a few weeks, he might possibly induce the fair Dora to transfer her affections, and her fortune, to him; in which case, an announcement of his engagement to the heiress, and a promise to pay directly after the marriage, would free him from all persecution. So, two days before the dinner party, the Honourable George Mullingar arrived ·at the Castle, much to the disgust and annoyance of Mr. John Smith, who had persuaded his father to let him off work, for a few days, at the office, that he might accept the pressing invitation extended to him by Miss Morton, to stay at Loombe. Smith thought he would have it all his own way this time; and, for the first three days of his visit, seemed to make great progress in the affections of his charmer, and he fondly hoped before the week was out, he might venture to pop the question, with great chance of success. Imagine then, his horror and vexation, on coming down to breakfast, the next morning, to learn that the Honourable George Mullingar was expected that afternoon, and to see the look of triumph and expectation that lit up the fair Dolly's countenance, at the thought of the new visitor's arrival. Directly after the humiliation and disappointment Lord Booby's conduct had caused her, the Parvenu's daughter had been glad to console herself with the attention of the young Solicitor, who she really liked better than any other of her would-be suitors, but, false pride, and anxiety to rise above her station, still gained the ascendancy, and directly she heard that the Earl's son was coming to Loombe, she determined to keep young Smith, as she called it, in his place, and carefully avoid giving him an opportunity of pressing his suit. Smith instantly discovered the change in his hostess's demeanour, and shrewdly suspected the reason, so, having too much sense to submit to being made a cat's-paw of a second time, and not really caring for the girl, or wishing to marry her, except for the advantage such an alliance would prove to him in a worldly point of view, John Smith determined to make a formal proposal at once, to old Morton, and then openly demand an interview with Miss Dora, before the expected guest's arrival, and if she again refused to lend a willing ear to his entreaties, he would leave her house, and abandon all thoughts of her. Accordingly about twelve o'clock, Miss Dora having refused to walk out with him as on previous mornings, the young man tapped at the door of old Morton's sanctum, and found him lolling in an arm-chair, with the newspaper on his knee, but half asleep through the heat and drowsy state of the atmosphere, on the warm August morning. He roused up, however, quickly on Smith's entrance, and lent a willing ear to his suit, for the old man felt that, however much he and Dora wished to "cultivate" the nobility, and those above them, that his child's happiness would be better secured by a marriage with one in her own station, and the Booby episode had caused him such horror and disgust, that he would be thankful to see Dora safely wedded to one he could trust, and who held so respectable a position as the young solicitor.

"Well, Smith," he said, "I loike you and respect you, and your good folk, and I believe you'd make a good 'usband to my dear gal. I'm sure you've given proof you love 'er, by asking a second time, so if she's willing, I'll give my consent and blessing, and a tidy sum to 'elp to keep the pot boiling, you know," he added, with a wink and a benignant grin. Off rushes the lawyer, delighted, and meeting Dora on the stairs, will put up with no excuses, but insists on an interview, in which he endeavours to simulate an ardour and passion he does not really feel, tells her that his whole happiness depends on her, that he cannot live without her, and reminding her of his constancy and devotion, as he kneels at her feet, implores her to give him a word, a look, of encouragement.

Dolly, whose vanity makes her believe all he says, and who really likes the young man, is touched in spite of herself, and half inclined to give him a favourable answer, but the thought of the Honourable George, and the hope that *he* might be in time dazzled by her charms, and give her his name and high position, overcame her better feelings, and she said:

"Pray rise, Mr. Smith, and forgive me, if I am unable at present to accept your most flattering proposal. If you will allow me, I will think over it, but there must be no engagement between us. I cannot so easily recover the annoyance and ill-treatment I received from Lord Booby as to give my word already to another suitor," she added in excuse.

"But surely, Miss Morton, you don't want his Lordship to think you are inconsolable? Why not give me the right to protect you against such as he? Come, dear," said John Smith, insinuatingly stealing an arm round Dora's plump form, and trying to draw her towards him, "your father has given his consent; I know your brother would not object; come, make me the happiest man by saying Yes!"

"La, Mr. Smith, how you do go on to be sure," said Dolly, wavering, and allowing him to kiss her, for Dora Morton was not a woman who thought there was any harm in a kiss, with or without an engagement. Unlike our Meg, her sister-in-law, who, though only a lady's-maid before her marriage, had the refinement and purity of ideas that caused her, though loving Tom Morton, to refuse her lips until she made up her mind to give him her heart, Dora had no such scruples, and, as she liked the young man, she considered there was no objection to a few mild love passages between them, but she strenuously objected to an engagement, and defied all Smith's endeavours to obtain a decided answer. At last she promised that in a week's time she would finally make up her mind, and Smith, notwithstanding the experience he had gained in his profession, could not believe that any girl could be so double-faced, as partly to encourage one man, whilst she thought of trying to catch another, and was fain to be content for the moment, as he strolled leisurely at her side through the beautiful grounds that surrounded the Castle, fondly hoping that ere long, as Dora's husband, he would possess a share of the wealth so lavishly displayed.

At last came the moment anxiously looked forward to by Dora, as the large carriage, that had been despatched to the station, returned, conveying the Honourable George Mullingar in its roomy depths. The dapper little figure jumped out, and eagerly bent over Miss Dora's hand, murmuring the joy he felt in again approaching one so charming. Dora blushed and simpered, whilst Smith wished the new comer at the bottom of the sea, and determined bravely to stand his ground, and not make way for the Earl's son, at the lady's side. He scowled at the youth, and tried hard the next day to pick a quarrel with him, but George Mullingar, with all his faults, was too much of a gentleman to have a row with one of his host's guests, and only treated Smith's impertinence with a well-bred stare. Dora, however, was highly indignant, and spoke her mind so plainly to the country lawyer that he took his departure in a huff, and left the wealthy heiress free to bestow her hand and money (as he told her) on any fortune-hunting aristocrat she pleased.

Dolly cared little for his anger; at the present moment, all her thoughts and time were engaged by the attentions of the Honourable George, who lost no opportunity of ingratiating himself into the favour of his hostess and her father. Old Morton was not at all pleased at the Solicitor's second dismissal, and reprimanded his daughter sharply about the way she had treated him, but, as usual, Dolly got over the old man's better sense, and had her own way in the end. And so matters stood when the day of the grand dinner party arrived, at which the Honourable George Mullingar was to be introduced to all the best county families, when Miss Dora fondly hoped he would continue to shew her the marked attention he had done since his arrival, and make such an exhibition of his sentiments that he would feel bound in honour to propose afterwards. Her heart swelled with pride and delight, as she thought of the proud position she would occupy, as the Honourable Mrs. George Mullingar, and of the still higher title that loomed for her in the distance.

The Earl's son wished no better than for his attentions to the heiress to be remarked, and indeed as soon as possible to assume the *rôle* of *fiancé* to her. Unlike Lord Booby, who, for reasons we may imagine, shunned publicity, George Mullingar was only anxious to court it, and though he feared a row with his mother for contemplating so plebeian an alliance, he knew well enough that the noble Earl would wink at the lady's low origin and vulgarity for the sake of her gold. The Earl was a poor man, and his son's allowance sadly drained his slender income, added to which the young man was constantly begging for little extra tips.

"Gad, governor!" he used to say with

his languid drawl. "Mess expenses are enawmuth. A man can't live in our doothid exthpenthif wedgement without hunting," etc. So George made desperate love to the rosy Dora, and, as he sat alone with her over five-o'clock tea, he took her plump, podgy fingers in his slim, aristocratic palm, and said, "Dear Miss Morton, won't you give your fond admiwrer some encouwragement? Oh, Dowra! lovely Dowra! say you have gwrown to cawre a little for one who pwrays for you, and whose evewry thought is full of love and adowration for your sweet self."

And Dolly, again dazzled by the thought of the rank she would possess, listened to his prayers and protestations of eternal devotion, and promised to be his. Old Morton, in his heart, would have preferred the humble Smith, believing he would make the best and truest husband; but Dolly, as before, over-persuaded him, and he gave a reluctant consent, just before the august company invited to the dinner-party were expected.

Lord and Lady Burnside arrived from Berwick in their grand barouche, with their crest showily emblazoned on either side, and their tall, powdered coachman and footman. Sir John and Lady Hammond, and their daughter, came from ten miles north of the Tweed; then an old maid, the Lady Anne Lanark, a prim, stiff-necked specimen of humanity, they say she had once been a fashionable beauty, and greatly courted in society, but she thought, with her beauty and rank, she ought not to marry any one lower than a duke or an earl, and so refused the rising young doctor that courted and really loved her, and would have gladly married her, notwithstanding her slender dowry.

But dukes and earls are not so plentiful, or so easily caught, by almost portionless maidens, however beautiful they may be, and the lovely Anne Lanark had flirted and languished, season after season, till she gradually became a wizened, shrivelled-up old woman, as thin as a thread paper and as sour as a bit of lemon-peel. Dora had invited another county magnate and his wife; but that very morning the lady had sent an excuse saying she had a return of bronchitis, from which she so often suffered. *Entre nous*, this fair dame's bronchial attacks invariably came on when she was engaged to a dinner at the Castle. Sir Charles, and Lady Leslie, and their son, had also received an invitation; but poor Leonora was in no state for dining out, or, indeed, going out at all, and Tony was away in Switzerland, though he had been telegraphed for on account of his mother's illness, and was daily expected. Dr. Grey, and Ellen, and Frank Meredith joined the party, also a young curate from a fashionable church near Belgrave Square, where the Mortons had a pew, and attended during their visits to London. The Reverend Augustus Parker was younger brother to Lord Burnside, and was thought much of in London society. He wrote annually reams of the best-intentioned, and most vapid sermons, and might be tracked across the country by little "awakening" pamphlets, at one and sixpence per hundred, which dribbled from his pockets as he journeyed along. Two days after his stay at the Castle, Ellen, when visiting some of the poor cottagers, found one old woman had received a copy of "The Road to Heaven," by the Reverend Augustus Parker, whilst the village grocer had been favoured with a sheaf of "Satan, Beware," by the same author.

Such was the party gathered together to meet the Honourable George Mullingar, who was speedily introduced as Miss Dora's *fiancé* to all assembled. Ellen and Dr. Grey looked grave as they thought of the interrupted wedding a month ago, and wondered how the cotton spinner's daughter could so easily transfer her affections from one man to another, and could now premise her hand to such a boy. They knew nothing of the flirtation with young Smith a few days ago; of the offer he had made her, and the half acceptance of it, and the tender passages that had ensued between them; but, to their honest, homely minds, the fact that a girl could so quickly take up, and actually engage herself to any man, so soon after the unpleasant and humiliating scene at the Hanover Square Church, was both amazing and revolting. Meredith, who was better versed in the ways of society, and who estimated Miss Dora at her proper worth, grinned as he looked at the lovers, and thought of all the stories of the debts and escapades of the Earl's son that he had so frequently heard circulated at clubs and in the world generally. But it was no affair of his; though, when he thought of the probable misery that would arise from such a marriage, and the trouble and annoyance it might cause to the poor old Parvenu, and to good, honest Tom, for whom Frank had the strongest feelings of friendship and respect, he felt half inclined to say a word of warning. He finally determined to write privately to Tom, telling him all he had heard of the young lieutenant, and advising him to make inquiries before his sister was further compromised. However, before Tom had time to attend to this good advice, or even answer the letter, an event occurred which rendered his interference unnecessary. The news of Dora's engagement spread like wild-fire in the neighbourhood, and soon became the subject of conversation in every shop and cottage for miles distant, whilst a universal titter ran round amidst the gentry and better classes, all of whom had read of the scene at St. George's, Hanover Square, or had been invited on that interesting occasion. Young Smith was furious, and wrote a violent letter to the fair Dora, who only shrugged her fat shoulders, after she perused it, and consigned it instantly to the flames.

Dolly was quite herself again, and believed that, at last, she had secured the prize of an aristocratic husband, who would give her the position in society she felt she would so highly adorn. Poor Dolly! Many is the slip between the cup and the lip! Whilst leisurely sauntering in the grounds of the Castle, three days after your dear George's arrival, and listening to the pretty speeches, and inane flattery he poured into your ears, two rough-looking men advanced towards your lover, and laying a hand on each arm, arrested him in the Queen's name, not only for debt, but forgery, and insisted on his accompanying] them instantly to London.

Soon after, the Honourable George Mullingar's crime was the talk of the town, though the poor old Earl, his father, had tried hard to save him from public ignominy, and had offered all he possessed, to hush up the affair, but the brother officer whose name he had taken, would listen to no inducement, or entreaty; the society papers made much of the trial, whilst each incident of the young scapegrace's past life, was quickly brought to light, and extracts from the dailies, were printed in large letters, and stretched on the pavement, in the vicinity of the Clubs in St. James's and Pall Mall. Then a portrait of the heiress, and would-be bride, with a double caricature of old Morton, first as the poor factory lad, and then as the rich and portly cotton lord, appeared in the shop windows in the Strand, and public thoroughfares, with a picture of the Law Court on the day of the trial, and photograph of the prisoner at the bar. Then no sooner had the sentence against him been pronounced than sandwich men paraded the streets, with placards from Madame Tussaud's, announcing life-sized figure of the Honourable George Mullingar as convicted of forgery, and sentenced to transportation and penal servitude, on view daily, being the last addition to the Chamber of Horrors, at the celebrated wax-work exhibition in Marylebone Road.

So ended Miss Dora's second engagement, and so, for this story we must leave her, to hide her discomfiture in silence and solitude, and after a time, gratefully accept her brother and Meg's charitable invitation to stay a few weeks at their Lancashire home, and thus avoid, for a short space, the neighbourhood in which she had acquired so unenviable a notoriety.

CHAPTER XI.

HOW DARE YOU, VILLAIN, USE MY MOTHER'S NAME?

LADY LESLIE's attendant, Kitty, had been severely reprimanded by Sir Charles, when she returned home alone, the day she had been so annoyed by the little Luigi, and much anxiety had been felt, until the boy arrived safely an hour later, when the girl was warned that, if she were not more careful in future, she would lose her place. So, when Kitty called the child, to dress him for early dinner, a few days later, and discovered that he was nowhere to be found, great was her dismay and trouble. She incautiously went to her mistress' room, enquiring if Master Luigi were there, and frightened Leonora by saying the boy was missing.

The poor mother's anxious heart was quickly alarmed, and she rose in haste, and tried to walk to the door, but a giddy faintness seized her and bound her again to the couch. Tony, who had just arrived, and was sitting with his mother, said all he could to soothe her, and told her there was no cause for alarm, for the boy often ran about alone close to the house, and he would go and find him and bring him up to her. Long did Tony search, aided by Sir Charles, and loudly did they call the boy by name, but no success rewarded their efforts, and after an hour, when they, with old Curtis and the footman, had explored every portion of the grounds, the father and son returned to the house, hoping he might have come back during their absence. But no; the frightened maids met them at the entrance with the intelligence that the child was still missing, and old Maggie ran hastily down, begging Sir Charles to go up to his wife, and try to calm her, for she feared the effect the fright and anxiety might have on her weak frame.

The Baronet went up kindly to Leonora, and said all in his power to comfort her, but she, remembering Varani's determination to have the boy, told the Squire she believed he had stolen him, and that she should never see him again, whilst the tears streamed down her poor wan cheeks, and she sobbed in anguish. The Squire was at his wits' end, and at a loss what to do for the best. He dreaded leaving his wife whilst she was so fearfully excited, and feared, in her weak state, the consequences to her, yet he felt it his duty to institute a more thorough search for her child, though he had too low an opinion of Varani to believe he would saddle himself with the boy. At last he determined to let Tony and the young footman go off beyond the grounds to search and make inquiries in the neighbourhood, whilst he remained at home to guard Leonora from any sudden fright or danger. Just as they were starting, however, Jim the groom arrived from Berwick, where he had been to fetch a young horse that the Squire had lately purchased, and gave them the startling intelligence that, as he approached the station, he met a fly, evidently coming from it, and being driven at a furious pace, and that, as it dashed past him, to his amazement he saw Master Luigi seated inside, with a dark, foreign looking gentleman. As the child looked quite contented and happy, the groom thought it was all right, and supposed he had gone with a friend of his father's, and took no further trouble about it until he heard at the Manor of the consternation and alarm caused by the boy's absence. Whilst they were discussing the best plan to pursue, Meredith returned from the Vicarage, and instantly offered to accompany Tony in his search, and the two young men started, declaring they would not return without the child.

After they left, a messenger was dispatched for Dr. Quin, and another begging the Vicar and Ellen to come instantly to the Manor, as both Sir Charles and old Maggie were greatly alarmed at the state of nervous excitement into which Lady Leslie had been thrown. Dr. Quin looked grave, but gave his patient a composing draught, and Ellen sat by her couch, holding her hand, and bathing her forehead, until the opiate she had swallowed took effect, and she closed her eyes in a feverish, troubled sleep, whilst Dr. Grey remained with Sir Charles, who in his anguish at last confided all his past troubles to his good faithful old friend, asking his advice and assistance in the strait in which he was placed. The kind Vicar listened with pain and grief to the sad story of crime and unhappiness that had darkened his friend's life, and he felt sincere compassion for the poor woman who had sinned, and whose life had been ruined through her mother's wicked deceit. He said all he could to soften Sir Charles' heart towards her, and to prepare him for the last parting, for Dr. Quin had assured him that she *could not* live many weeks, but that any violent sorrow or excitement might cause almost immediate decease, in the weak state she was now in.

At last the Squire believed that his wife's death was imminent, and as he gradually realised the blow that was about to fall on him, his strong self-contained nature gave way, and his grief was terrible to behold. After a time, the

Vicar's kind words and exhortations calmed the first outburst of his sorrow, and he crept softly to Leonora's room, and kneeling at her bed-side, inwardly vowed that henceforth, while he lived, no reproach or harsh word towards her should escape him; Sir Charles Leslie was a good man, and, notwithstanding his wife's faults, he had been deeply attached to her, and now that he felt she was fading from his sight, the old tenderness returned with renewed force, and he forgot all but the love he had borne her in the first happy years of their married life. In the mean while, Meredith and Tony had arrived at the village station, and were instantly informed that the little Luigi had left two hours ago for Berwick, accompanied by a tall, dark, foreign-looking man; that, as the child seemed happy and was chattering away unconcernedly in Italian, the station master and porters of course thought it was all right, and that the gentleman was some Italian friend or relation of Lady Leslie.

Frank Meredith dispatched a messenger to Sir Charles Leslie, telling him the direction the fugitives had taken, and saying that he and Tony were starting in pursuit.

Count Varani had been much distressed and horrified, when the news of his foster brother's death and the sad shipwreck had reached his ears, and it had greatly upset his plans, for, before his quarrel with the Jesuit, it had been arranged that the same vessel should convey him and the boy, and (as to the last, he fondly hoped

Leonora also) to a foreign port. Now he was without assistance, and his slender means had been terribly reduced by the expenses of his sojourn in London and the North. He had counted over his small stock of money the night before, and found that it was only with the strictest economy he could eke out sufficient to live on, and pay travelling fares etc., till he reached Italy, so he had determined on taking the cheap steamer from Newcastle to Antwerp, and then going southwards by slow trains, in which he could obtain third-class tickets, and thus reach Venice. But his great object at present was to baffle pursnit, as soon as the little Luigi had consented to accompany him, so on arriving at Berwick he took a fly to a little station on the road to Newcastle, where he despatched his small valise for that port, and then determined to tramp across country, so that all track of him and the boy might be lost, getting an occasional lift in a waggon or cart till he reached the sea-port town, whence he would depart instantly in the steamer. When Luigi had left the Manor, young Antonio Leslie had not arrived, and Meredith was as usual with Ellen at the Vicarage, so Varani did not count on the two young men's energy and activity in the pursuit. Meredith, who (as we know) had overheard the conversation between Lady Leslie and the Count, though from his enforced hiding-place he had not been able to see the latter, shrewdly suspected who had stolen the boy, but Tony was profoundly ignorant, and had not for years even heard the name of Varani, and certainly never in any way connected him with the estrangement he could not help noticing between his parents, and that had long so greatly pained the honest, affectionate lad, so they had not much guide in enquiring for and tracking the fugitive, as even Meredith could give no description of the man; but on arriving at Berwick they soon discovered the fly spoken of by Jim, that had conveyed the Italian and the little boy to the neighbouring station and had just returned, so, jumping into it, they ordered the coachman to drive back there, at full speed. At this little station they were informed that a man accompanied by a boy, had despatched a portmanteau by rail to Newcastle, but had not gone by train; on further inquiry, a porter remembered he had asked the road to Newcastle, evidently with the intention of starting in that direction. In the month of August, tourists and pedestrians were so common in that part, that the fact of the luggage being sent on, and the travellers preferring the excursion on foot, elicited no surprise or remark. Hiring a fresh horse and trap, on went Meredith and Tony along the high road to Newcastle, till they came to the small village inn, the "Blue Bell" at Belford, about half way between Berwick and Alnwick; here they halted to gain further information, and were soon told that a traveller, with a little boy, had enquired the road to Newcastle, and had been pointed out the short cut over the mountains to Alnwick; that the child had complained of fatigue, and that a miller had offered both him and his father a ride in his cart as far as where the path branched off from the high road.

"His father?" exclaimed Antonio, "Why he is Sir Charles Leslie's youngest son, my brother! Pray who is it that has stolen the poor boy and dares to call him his son?"

"Well, sir," said the innkeeper, "*he* did not say the child was his son, but we all noticed such a strong resemblance between them, that I concluded such was the relationship."

"Could it be my uncle, Francesco Marchetta?" said the youth to Meredith, "but no, it is impossible! He would have come straight to the house, and surely would not have caused my poor mother such sorrow and anxiety as to take the child out without her knowledge and consent."

"Well," interrupted Meredith, "let us lose no more time. We ought soon to catch them up, and regain possession of the boy!" Off again went the young men, leaving the dog-cart they had hired to wait for them on the high road, and starting at a round pace along the narrow footpath described as the short cut. Count Varani had met his child that morning as had been arranged between them, and had persuaded him after some little difficulty to accompany him. Leonora had been so weak and ill for the last few days, that Luigi had been kept from her as much as possible, the doctor and attendants having noticed that she was always more excited and feverish after he had been with her. The boy resented this, and became still more sulky and ill-tempered, doing all in his power to aggravate and worry his attendant, Kitty, who detested him, and on her side took no pains to conceal her dislike or to make friends; so the child was far from happy at home, and hailed Varani's proposal to go off with him to Italy with delight. But now, after a few hours, as the boy became footsore and weary, and missed the good dinner and tender care he had always received, he began to repent, and upbraid Varani for having lured him away from home, and threaten to leave him and go back.

Varani did all in his power to soothe and please the child, and half carried him along the path, promising that directly they reached the next village he should soon have nice food, and a conveyance should be hired to take them on. And so, amidst

Luigi's grumblings and complaints, the journey was continued, and they had just arrived at the brow of a hill when voices behind them were heard crying, "Halt! halt!" and Tony and Meredith rushed forward. Paolo Varani's fierce temper was aroused at the idea of pursuit, and he determined he would not allow the boy to be recaptured. The thought of all that might ensue if he also were taken, and the hatred with which the sight of Sir Charles Leslie's son inspired him, warped his better nature, and hastily in fury drawing a pistol from his pocket, he levelled it at Antonio, as the youth advanced, and fired! A low moan, followed by an exclamation of horror, was immediately heard, and Varani, to his terror and consternation, saw the baronet's son bending over the prostrate form of the little Luigi! The child, on seeing his brother, had rushed forward just as the Italian fired, and, intercepting the shot, received a deadly wound in his back, that severed the spinal cord, and killed him on the spot.

"Oh mio bambino! Mio bambino! Ah maledetto!" cried Varani in anguish, falling on his knees and bending over the child, frantically feeling his little body, and discovering that already his heart had ceased to beat. "Ah Leonora, adorata mia Leonora! Is it thus I have fulfilled your sacred trust?"

"How dare you, villain, use my mother's name? How dare you insult her?" exclaimed Antonio, furiously turning on Varani with menacing accents, whilst Meredith, who had a slight knowledge of surgery, examined the poor child, and soon saw that no human skill could bring back the little life already extinguished. As the awful fact that the boy was dead became evident to Antonio, he glared at Varani and cried, "You have failed in your villainous attempt to murder me! Instead my poor little innocent brother has fallen your victim! Who are you? Why should you steal the child and try to compass my death?"

"Hush, both of you," said Meredith gravely, as he laid a hand on each. "Rise, Count Varani, you are my prisoner, until I hear Sir Charles Leslie's wishes respecting you. Do not add to your crimes by speaking of the past," he said in a low voice. "Think what you would do," he added imploringly, as the fear struck him lest

Tony should learn his mother's shame, and lest disgrace should ensue to the squire through Varani's arrest and the child's death.

"Nay, Frank, this is my affair," cried Tony, who had again examined poor Luigi's lifeless body. "This man shall answer to me for murdering my brother. Speak out, sirrah! I will try and be patient and hear all you have to say."

"Let me pass!" said Varani, fiercely, "or it will be worse for you! My child is dead! I care not to bandy words with Sir Charles Leslie's son!"

"Your child? Again you dare to say so?" exclaimed Antonio, whose temper was now fairly roused, as, in spite of Meredith's entreaty and intervention, he furiously rushed on the Count, intending to knock him down. But neither Tony or Frank, unarmed, were a match for Count Varani, who, quickly drawing a dagger from his breast, dashed first at Meredith's detaining hand, and then half buried his weapon in the youth's body, giving him, as he thought, a deadly wound. Then, springing over his prostrate foe, and shaking himself free from the young barrister, as he cast one regretful glance at the poor child's corpse, Varani fled.

Meredith, who had received a deep gash on the left arm, from which blood was oozing through his coat sleeve, twisted his handkerchief as tightly as he could round the wounded member, as he knelt in terror by his friend's side.

Antonio was insensible, but to Meredith's relief still breathed. Varani's dagger had entered his ribs on the right side, and the life-blood seemed to be pouring from him. Frank hastily half tore off his clothes till he came to a deep gash, and knew that unless he could staunch the bleeding his friend would soon perish. He tore part of the youth's linen and part of his own into strips and bound up the wound, and then looked round despairingly. No help was near. What could he do? He raised Tony's head on his arm and moistened his lips with a little brandy from a small pocket flask he had had the precaution to bring with him, and tried to make him swallow a few drops. Gradually his efforts were rewarded, consciousness returned, and the poor lad opened his eyes.

"My mother! oh, my poor mother!" were Antonio's first words, as his eyes fell on the dead body of the little Luigi, and a remembrance of all that had happened floated mistily before him. "The shock will kill her! Has the villain escaped?" he added, trying to rise, but instantly sinking back exhausted.

"Yes, dear," said Meredith, soothingly. "I could not detain him, for I too am hurt, and it was as much as I could do to bind up your wound. And now I must leave you and try to get assistance, or we shall both perish." As he spoke, Meredith tried to rise from the kneeling posture he had assumed whilst tending his friend, but a giddiness came over him from loss of blood, and with dismay he discovered that, whilst he was so intent on binding up Tony's wound, his own had again opened. Making a supreme effort, he swallowed a little brandy, then, leaving the flask with Tony, and bidding him keep up his courage and wait patiently his return, Frank pressed his uninjured hand tightly on his bleeding arm, and dragged himself away.

Nervous about Antonio, who he doubted that he should ever again see alive, horror-stricken at the thought of the little Luigi's murder, and the blow it would cause his poor mother, faint and ill, and scarcely able to force himself along, Frank was in a sorry plight, but the thought of his sweet Ellen's distress if anything befell him, and the intense longing to be again with her, supported him and gave him renewed energy.

On he crawled towards the high road, where he had left the dog-cart, calling out loudly as he went for help and succour.

But no voice answered. The path led through a lone, though beautiful valley, where the wild brake closed on either side, so, unless any other traveller chanced to be journeying that way, there was little hope of Meredith's being seen or heard. It was a lovely spot; honeysuckle, hawkweed, and pink and white convolvulus varied the soft verdure of the thicket; whilst the view of a neighbouring brook, rippling in the sunshine, and chequered at intervals by the rich weeds floating on the surface, interspersed with delicate grasses and silver water-lilies, added enchantment to the scene. Tall trees, with a prodigal variety of hues, stood in the distance; blue, purple, yellowing tints, with a deep mass of verdure frowning into the darkest green, and broken again into hundreds of minor subtler shades, as the bright August sun pierced the foliage, throwing a warmer light upon some favoured glade. But poor Meredith was in no state to admire the beauties of nature; his one hope was to gain assistance and succour for Tony and himself, whilst he had strength to pursue his way; but his limbs tottered, and could scarcely support his weight, and he began to despair, when an answering shout to his cries for help was heard, and an old Scotch pedlar, carrying a pack strapped on his back, emerged on the pathway, and quickly advanced towards him.

"Why friend," said the old man (hastily supporting Frank, and forcing him to sit down on the grass), "ye seem in a sair plight, and no fit to gang yer way, and covered with blude frae top to toe."

"Help! help for my friend," said Frank

faintly, as the pedlar hastily unstrapped and opened his pack, and taking a small bottle containing a cordial from it, forced him to swallow it before speaking further. Then, as Meredith gained sufficient strength to explain how sadly he stood in need of assistance, and how alarmed he was lest his friend should die whilst he had left him seeking aid, the old pedlar put a whistle to his lips and blew a shrill blast, hoping to attract the attention of some other good Samaritan, who might be found in that part, but none answered his call.

After binding up Frank's wound, and leaving him to rest and recover his strength whilst he guarded the pack, the old man started off at a round pace for assistance, promising to hasten all in his power, and bring men, and if possible a doctor, to help in removing him and the friend for whose safety he was so anxious. Meanwhile, Tony, left alone, faint and giddy from the loss of blood, and suffering great agony from the deep wound in his side, believed his last hour had come. The last few months, and the blow he had suffered when Ellen refused him, added to his present grief at his mother's ill-health, had worked their change upon Antonio's face. The bright, joyous glance had settled into calm. He conversed more rarely than before, and though his manner was as affectionate, and his smile as kindly, the smile was more thoughtful, and the kindness had forgot its passion. He had to all outward appearance subdued a love that was so early crossed, but not the faithful remembrance, that caused Ellen still to be dearer to him than all others, and seemed to forbid him to replace the image he had graven upon his heart. Now, as he lay between life and death, too weak and in too great agony to move, with the dead body of his poor little brother lying at his feet, the young girl's name was on his lips, and he thought of her, as well as of his dearly loved parents, as he sent inward prayers to Heaven for their well-being and comfort.

CHAPTER XII.

MY CHILD! MY CHILD!

THE old pedlar was as good as his word, and lost no time in reaching the dog-cart, in which, after explaining all he knew to the coachman, he was driven at a furious pace back to the inn, where his story created great alarm and consternation. Four men, with two hastily improvised stretchers, were quickly despatched, and a messenger was sent off for the village doctor, who accompanied the pedlar on his return in the dog-cart, whilst rooms were prepared for the sufferers, in case it was found necessary to detain them at

Belford. On reaching Meredith they found the pedlar's clever bandages had lasted well, and very little blood now came from the wound, so the young man felt stronger, and would have returned to his poor friend before their arrival, had he not feared to move lest they should miss them both. Now, however, after drinking a cup of wine, and hastily eating food they brought from the inn, nothing would induce Frank to remain behind, and he accompanied the cavalcade to where Antonio lay, for by this time the men with the stretchers had joined them. The Baronet's son lay quite still, so still that Meredith's heart at first gave a throb of anguish, for he thought all was over, but as they approached him the youth opened his eyes and glanced feebly at them.

The Doctor looked grave, as he examined the wound, and said he ought not to be moved, but as it was impossible to keep him in that desolate part, without a house near, or even a hut to shelter him, there was no help for it, so, after applying fresh bandages, and vainly endeavouring to persuade him to swallow food, they tenderly lifted him, notwithstanding his groans and entreaties to be left to die in peace, and, followed by the other stretcher bearing the poor child's corpse, the melancholy procession started, Meredith leaning on the Doctor's arm, and supported on the other side by the kind old Pedlar.

Long before reaching the inn, Tony had swooned again, and the Doctor had the gravest fears for his life, as, in spite of all the care taken, moving him had caused the bleeding to increase. On arriving at Belford, Meredith, whose presence of mind never deserted him, however great the emergency, sent off two telegrams, one to an eminent London surgeon, begging him to start instantly for Belford, to attend Sir Charles Leslie's son, who was lying there seriously wounded, the other to Tom Morton, imploring him to beg Meg to go instantly to Lady Leslie, as old Maggie must be despatched to Belford, to nurse Antonio.

The young barrister then thought of telegraphing to Sir Charles, but when he considered that the Manor was six miles from the station, and there migth be some delay in despatching the telegram from the little village of Loombe, he concluded that it was better to wait and break the intelligence gently to the Baronet, directly he arrived. Frank hesitated, and felt very uneasy at leaving his poor friend to the care of strangers, but he knew he could do him no good for a few hours, and he thought he was bound to return to the Manor, and tell the Squire all that had passed, added to which, Frank was severely wounded himself, and although his courage, and manly endurance, enabled him to keep up, and partly disguise the pain he suffered, he felt that he soon must have rest and quiet, or he would soon break down altogether.

So Meredith returned from the telegraph office to the little inn, and there made all possible arrangements for poor Tony's comfort. The Doctor promised not to leave his room till the London surgeon arrived, and the landlady, a kind, motherly old body, said she'd tend and nurse the poor young fellow as if he were her own son. The lad was still insensible, when Meredith hurried from the sick-room to catch the train, that was also to bear the little Luigi's dead body. The news of the accident that had taken place, soon spread over the little town, and the police inspector detained Frank till he had written down his deposition, in which the shrewd young lawyer said as little as possible, and completely ignored the murderer's name and position, alleging the hurried meeting and almost instantaneous shot that had been fired, and then the struggle in which both he and young Leslie were wounded, as an excuse for not being able accurately to describe the man who had committed the crime. Telegrams were sent off to all the seaport towns to arrest any suspicious-looking person, but without any description of the culprit, the police were at fault, and the chances of catching him were as remote, as Meredith fondly hoped they would be. Anyhow, he would do or say nothing without the Baronet's consent to assist in tracking a person whose arrest might cause such trouble and disgrace to those he so dearly loved and respected. After all these arrangements were completed, poor Frank was exhausted and looked so ill and suffering, for his wound was very painful, and he was quite unable to use his right arm, that the Belford Doctor would not allow him to return alone to Loombe, and insisted on sending his young assistant to take care of him and the little boy's corpse. The sun was setting, and a crimson glory pervaded the sky as the cab from the station conveying Frank Meredith and his ghastly charge arrived at the Manor. Frank, fearing lest Lady Leslie might see the poor child's body carried into the house, had decided to go round to the back entrance, leaving the corpse watched over by the Doctor's assistant, in the cab, until he had slightly prepared the domestics for the awful shock that awaited them, but Ellen's quick ears had caught the sound of wheels, and seeing the fly turn off to the servants' entrance, she flew after it, and was the first to greet her lover, as he slowly and painfully descended.

"Ellen," said Frank, before she had time to notice his altered appearance, "be brave, and come in quietly with me!"

"Oh Frank," cried the terrified girl, as she saw the arm supported by a sling and bandaged up, and the ashen hue that overspread her darling's face, "what dreadful accident has happened? You are hurt!"

"Dear Ellen," said the young man, as he threw his uninjured arm tenderly around her and drew her to his heart, "do not fret about me! I am wounded, darling, but not dangerously, and shall soon recover, but I bring bad news for Sir Charles and Lady Leslie, and I want my little Ellen to help me to break it to them."

"What is it?" said Ellen in a low grave voice. "Where is Tony?"

"Tony is wounded! He is at the Inn at Belford, but I hope will recover," added Meredith quickly, seeing the girl's look of terror and dismay, "but Luigi's state is worse. Be brave, darling! Let us keep our courage, and do all to help and comfort those who will suffer deeply. It must be broken gently to poor Lady Leslie. The boy she so dearly loved, is dead."

"Dead!" exclaimed Ellen horrified, and wringing her hands in despair. "Oh! what shall we do! It will kill his poor mother, weak and ill as she is! How did it happen?"

"Dear Ellen," said Frank gravely, "it is a sad story, and I will tell you some of it later, but don't ask questions just now. Call your father. Is he here?"

"Yes! Sir Charles begged him to stay till he returned, and he is sitting with old Maggie at Lady Leslie's bedside."

"Returned!" exclaimed Meredith, alarmed. "Where then has he gone?"

"Why? Did he not overtake you?" said Ellen. "As soon as your messenger arrived, saying you had learnt the direction the boy had been taken, Lady Leslie having succumbed to the effects of the sleeping draught, Sir Charles determined to follow you, and he must have caught the next train."

"Oh, Ellen," said Frank, "this makes me still more uneasy. Tell your father quietly to come here, that I may consult him immediately."

The girl ran off on this errand, whilst Frank told old Curtis of the child's death, and amidst the group of frightened and awe-stricken servants, the poor boy's body, already stiff and cold, was brought in and laid on a bench.

Tom Meredith turned to the young footman, and asked him to go off instantly and fetch Dr. Quin.

"Please, sir," said the man, "the doctor has been here this morning, and promised to look in again. Indeed, I expect him every minute."

"It is well," replied Frank, "then your mistress must not be told till he arrives." Meanwhile, Ellen went to Lady Leslie's room, and gently opening the door, without entering, whispered with a presence of mind wonderful for her years, "Father, I want you a minute; a messenger from home wishes to speak to you."

"Why, what is it, dear, is old Mrs. Price worse?" said the Vicar, thinking of an aged parishioner who was not expected to live many days, and going hastily to the door, but on glancing at Ellen's face and seeing her lips move, cautioning him to be quiet, the old man softly shut the door and walked with her along the passage, that old Maggie might not hear them, when Ellen told him, as gently as she could, of Luigi's death, and said Frank was wounded, and wanted to speak to him immediately. Dr. Grey was greatly shocked when the young barrister took him to an inner room, and told him all that had passed, and confided to him how much he knew of the sad history, that had led to these dire events, and asked him to advise him what to do for the best.

The old clergyman then told Meredith, in a few words, all that the Squire had confessed to him that morning, for as the young man knew so much, further concealment was useless, and both men felt and knew how implicitly they could trust each other to keep and guard the secret that had come to their knowledge. Both Meredith and Dr. Grey felt very uneasy about Sir Charles, for if he succeeded in reaching Varani, they feared that he also would be seriously wounded, if not killed.

They found Ellen kneeling by the poor little child's body when they returned to the servants' hall, the domestics standing round in fright and amazement. They cautioned all to keep perfectly quiet, and give no chance of Lady Leslie's hearing what had happened, until Sir Charles returned and had decided what should be done, and they begged Ellen to go back to Lady Leslie, who was still under the influence of the narcotics that had been administered to her, and to send old Maggie to them.

And now Meredith's strong active mind saw the necessity of immediate action. Laying his hand kindly on the Vicar's, he said : " Time presses, someone must be sent instantly to Belford to attend to Tony, and the poor little Luigi's body must be removed from the servants' hall." "Let it be brought to the library," said the Vicar. "Unhappy child! All that we can do to shield his poor mother must be done, and he must be buried as Sir Charles' own son."

Meredith first ordered the servants to bring the child's body to the library, to await Dr. Quin's arrival, when he feared an inquest must necessarily take place, and then he took old Maggie to an adjoining chamber, to tell her gently of the sad event, and request her to make her little preparations to start instantly to Belford, to pass the night there at poor Tony's bedside, and nurse him, and be present when the London surgeon that had been summoned should arrive. As Meredith quickly and calmly made all these arrangements, forgetting himself, and the injury he had suffered, in his deep anxiety to help his friends, his strength seemed suddenly to give way. Loss of blood and fatigue overcame him, and with a low moan, he fell forward in a deadly faint. Ellen, who had been left in charge of Lady Leslie, still asleep, hearing old Maggie's exclamation of distress, and fearing for her lover's safety, rushed out, and thus left the invalid for a few moments alone. Meanwhile the servants had brought in the dead body and laid it on a side table in the library, and Dr. Quin who had just arrived, after attending to Frank's arm and ordering him instantly to bed, was carefully examining the child's body, when the door suddenly opened, and to the horror and amazement of all present, Lady Leslie, exclaiming "My child! My child!" entered, and tottered towards the corpse. The Doctor and old Curtis hastily advanced to hide the ghastly sight from her view, but it was too late; she saw the stiff body, the little face, now rigid in death, and with a cry of anguish, fell forward on to her child, whilst a deep purple stream flowed from her mouth.

CHAPTER XIII.

HALT! OR I FIRE.

SIR CHARLES LESLIE had arrived at the little village station in time for the next train to that by which Tony and Meredith had travelled. He enquired at all the places along the line, and on hearing at Belford that the man and child, followed by the two young men, had taken the footpath to Alnwick, he determined to go on straight to the latter place, and then, if they had not arrived, he would start on the road back, and intercept them. Knowing the Italian's violent, vindictive temper, the

Squire felt very uneasy for his son's safety, and bitterly repented having allowed him to start on this dangerous errand. Feeling for the small pistol that he had taken the precaution to conceal in his breast-pocket before leaving the Manor, the Baronet, on arriving at Alnwick, and hearing that no one answering his description had been seen there, hastily started on the road back to Belford. He had walked about a mile, when all at once a quick step was heard, and suddenly rounding a corner, Count Varani almost ran up against him. To seize the pistol from his breast and point it at him was the Baronet's first idea, then as the remembrance of Leonora's grief struck him, he determined first to question the Italian as to where he had left the child. Varani recoiled amazed at the sight of Sir

Charles, then brandishing his dagger, stained already with poor Tony's blood, prepared to make a dash at him, but the Squire called out, "Halt, or I fire!" as he levelled the pistol at his head. Then, fixing his eye steadily on him he said, "Villain, where is the child?"

"Beyond your reach," answered Varani, "and where his step-brother will soon join him."

"What do you mean, Sirrah," replied the Baronet. "Have you seen my son?"

"Ah, that I have," said Paolo fiercely; "I would advise you to look after *him*, instead of threatening me."

"What mean you?" said the Squire, horrified. "Surely you have not injured him! Wretch, is it not enough that you will have killed as well as ruined the poor woman who loved you? Have you murdered her son also?"

"If he chose to fight *me*, it was no fault of mine if *he* had the worst of it, and was he not *your* flesh and blood, and therefore hateful to me?"

"Villain!" said the Baronet, "give up that dagger and surrender, or I fire. You shall not escape me this time, for the law shall deal with you."

"Oh, indeed! you would appeal to the law would you? All right! I ask no better; I can then give publicity to your dastardly act in stealing my affianced bride."

"You lie, Sirrah!" exclaimed Sir Charles, "for you well knew that when I married my unhappy wife I was quite ignorant of her attachment and engagement to you. *You* have destroyed her happiness and peace

Cannot you leave her alone now she is dying?"

"And pray whose fault is it she is dying?" retorted Varani. "As I told you before, you alone are her murderer."

"Peace, villain, or I fire," said Sir Charles, at last irritated beyond endurance.

"Oh! you'd slay me! then you wish your fine name to be dragged through the mud, and held up to scorn, do you?" retorted the Italian. "Fire if you will! I care not for my life! you have robbed my of all I held dear! You took from me the only woman I ever loved; sorrow and despair will soon now have done their work in killing her. I care not what you do with me, but whether you fire or shoot me on this spot, or whether you give me over to your infernal country's laws, your shame will be proclaimed, and at last that will avenge me!" So saying, Varani boldly threw down his dagger, and crossing his arms on his breast, stood unprotected before him.

Sir Charles lowered the pistol, and thus addressed him:—"Base seducer and profligate, I will not ruin my poor wife's name and memory by giving you the chance of injuring her! Go! Leave my sight for ever! May your own conscience be your punishment. Go! and repent, and may the Lord have mercy on your soul, and forgive the bitter misery you have caused in this world. But first tell me where is the boy? And where is my poor son, Antonio?"

"Follow that side path and you will

find both," said Varani, as he turned, picked up his dagger, and walked slowly and gloomily away, first looking again boldly and defiantly at the Squire.

Sick at heart, and with faltering steps, Sir Charles followed the little pathway till he came to a spot where two separate pools of blood bore witness to the desperate struggle that had taken place, but no trace of the boys, living or dead, were visible. On closely examining the ground, he saw the mark of many footsteps, and faintly hoping that succour had arrived in time, and that perhaps his beloved son was still alive, he walked on hastily to Belford, and arrived at the Inn where Antonio lay insensible, just after Meredith and the little Luigi's body had left for Loombe. The good folks at the hotel soon told all they knew of the accident that had happened, and said that Meredith also was severely wounded, but that before leaving, he had telegraphed for the London surgeon, and had promised to send someone that night to nurse the sufferer. So Sir Charles despatched a telegram to Dr. Grey saying he was safe, and should remain with Tony until the surgeon arrived, and left it to him and Dr. Quin to tell poor Lady Leslie as much as was absolutely necessary. Then remembering Meg's promise of going to her former mistress if she seriously needed her, feeling what a comfort she would be to his wife, and ignorant that Meredith had already thought of this, he also wired to Lancashire, imploring the faithful girl to go to the Manor without delay.

CHAPTER XIV.

THE LAST HOUR.

Sir Charles, having seen the London surgeon, and heard that Tony's wound, though dangerous, and requiring the greatest care and quiet, was not a fatal one, left soon after old Maggie's arrival, fearing from her account that he might not reach Loombe in time to see his poor wife again alive.

Dr. Grey met his old friend on his arrival at the Manor, and gave him a telegram from Tom Morton, saying that he and Meg had started, and would be at

Loombe early in the evening. He also told him that the old Marchesa had arrived from Venice, and with Ellen was watching at her daughter's bedside; that Leonora lay half-insensible, but had swallowed a little milk and brandy they had poured down her throat.

Dr. Grey then said that Frank Meredith had a painful, though not dangerous wound, and that the Doctor had forced him to go to bed, but that he prayed the Squire to go up to see him as soon as he arrived, having something very important to communicate. The Baronet instantly directed his steps to the young man's room, before even going to Lady Leslie.

"Why, Frank," he said, "this is a bad job, you wounded also, and suffering for all the trouble you have taken, and solicitude shown towards all my family. Old fellow, I am indeed grieved. Are you in much pain?"

"How is Tony?" replied Meredith anxiously; "my wound is but slight, but Tony, dear Tony, how is he?"

"Going on well; and the surgeon thinks he will recover," replied the Squire; "and now what is it you have to say to me?"

"Sir Charles, I scarcely like confessing it; but the day you suddenly returned from Berwick and surprised Lady Leslie speaking to a stranger in the grounds, I was at the spot, and was an unwilling listener to all that passed. I had climbed from the ruined wall to a small ledge beneath, to gather some beautiful specimens of wild ferns, thinking Ellen might like them, and delicacy prevented me from acknowledging my presence, thinking it might pain poor Lady Leslie, and I heard all that passed between her and Count Varani before you arrived, as well as the stormy scene between you and him. I longed to tell you and exonerate her from all present thought of evil, but feared your displeasure, and that I might perhaps do more harm than good, but now that they tell me she is dying, I can no longer keep silence, and I implore you to believe me, that had you heard all that passed between her and the Italian, you would not, you could not, have blamed her."

"Ah, Frank," said the Baronet, "you have discovered the secret misery of my life, and now try to shield the poor misguided woman who betrayed me; but you need not fear that I shall ever again show anger or harshness towards her; she is dying, and I can only remember how once I loved her, and that she is the mother of my dear son Tony."

"Charles," said Dr. Grey, quickly advancing, "you are still under a wrong impression. Frank heard Count Varani plead with your wife to fly with him; he heard her firm refusal, and the love she expressed to you and her children, declaring she would never leave you, but would, whilst she lived, endeavour to regain your esteem, and atone for the past."

"Did you really hear this Frank? Oh tell me! for pity's sake tell me all you know."

"Lady Leslie distinclly refused to listen to the man; upbraided him for continuing to persecute her, and told him she had discovered that your valet was his foster brother, meanly acting as spy over her movements."

"Giuseppe! my valet! Varani's foster brother!" exclaimed the Squire horrified, as many small incidents of the past came to his remembrance, and the truth seemed to flash across his mind.

"Yes! the man miserably drowned last week was Count Varani's foster brother, the Jesuit from Murano."

"Good heavens!" ejaculated the Baronet, "then he has been for months in my home, acting as a common spy and trying perhaps to frighten my poor wife, and threaten her, before committing the robbery we know of. Was she aware who he was?" added Sir Charles, quickly, still suspicious.

"She discovered it only the day before," replied Meredith, "and this caused the fresh attack you will remember she suffered; she told the Count how she had been insulted, insisted on his leaving her at once, and for ever, when apparently one of those terrible faintnesses seized her, and whilst weak and giddy, she was taking an eternal farewell of the Italian when you surprised them together."

"Thank God! then she was not again guilty," said Sir Charles solemnly, and then, as his heart smote him for the stern harsh way he had treated his suffering wife, and the thought struck him, that perhaps his conduct had hastened her death, the man's iron nature broke down, and turning to his old friend, he said, "Grey! I have sinned in doubting her; I have been cruel, unjust! Oh! tell me what I can do, guide me, teach me to act rightly. I would give my life to save hers!"

"I fear nothing can be done, Charles," replied Dr. Grey, "unless before her death she regains consciousness and you can soothe her last moments by the assurance of your love and forgiveness. Dr. Quin said she might live the night, or even through the next day, but recovery was hopeless. It was only a smaller vessel that broke, had it been a large one she would never have spoken again."

With uneven steps and tear-dimmed eyes, the Squire paced feverishly up and down the corridor leading to his wife's sick chamber, and his thoughts again wandered to the past, and the first happy days of his married life, before sin or doubt of Leonora's fidelity had entered his life. No one who saw the cold stern man, would have credited that emotion so soft, and yet so ardent, raged in his breast, or how intensely he realized the "all" that Leonora had been to him, and how bitter was the change her sin had caused in his life and character. Now, after Meredith's words had assured him that she was no longer faithless to him, and had tried so earnestly to do her duty, the old love returned with redoubled force, and he prayed for death that he might be with her in eternity. The tranquil rest, the shadow, the silence, the mere pause of the wheel of life, had no terror for him, could it join him to the woman he so fondly loved; could he feel the hope of eternal re-union in that "Invisible" beyond the stars. Is it not this thought which creates faith out of sorrow, and gives heavenly aspirations to the grieving heart, that before, in the possession of earthly joys, felt not the want of a divine power?

As the Squire watched for the passing away of the being more to him than all he possessed, and retraced the recollections of happy days passed beside her, now shadowed and mellowed down by time and sorrow, he felt what a world of hope would be buried in her grave! Then he thought anxiously of the possible capture of the man who had worked such deadly ruin, and of the disgrace and exposure that would ensue were he brought to a public trial. The police were already actively searching for him, and though Meredith had averred his inability to describe him, and Tony was as yet too ill for his deposition to be taken, there seemed small hope that the culprit would escape. The murder of the Baronet's supposed youngest son, and the dangerous wounding of the heir, created such horror and excitement in the neighbourhood, that the police redoubled their efforts. Detectives arrived from London, and every station, and every seaport, was watched narrowly. Sir Charles said nothing of his meeting with Varani, and Meredith still adhered to his statement, that in the hurry and confusion of the attack, and being so quickly wounded he did not notice the man suffi-

ciently to be able to describe him, and it
was not till three days later, when Antonio
being at last out of danger, was able to
give the police *his* version of the affair
that they received any guide, even as to
the murderer's personal appearance.

Sir Charles paused at the window in the
passage, and looked out at the calm summer
night; all was unutterably silent. Myriads
of stars shone in the heavens; the river
below flowed on in mighty calm, not a ripple
was seen in the waters; the moon girded
by thin fleecy clouds cast her shadows upon
rocks covered with verdure, and brought
the spire of the old church in the distance
into dim light. As he sorrowfully gazed at
the tranquil beauty of the scene before him,
a trembling hand was placed on his arm,
and starting, he beheld the old Marchesa

Marchetta. He turned courteously, as was his wont, and seeing the agony and distress, depicted on her countenance, as she said imploringly, " Can you ever forgive me?" he placed an arm tenderly around her, and bending over the silver hair, implanted a kiss on her forehead, and said:

" You have much to forgive me also, for I could not make your darling happy, or even keep her alive. Dear Marchesa," he added, " do not weep! She is going to a brighter, a better world, let us pray that we may all be re-united in Heaven, where no earthly sins, or impure thoughts can enter, to mar our perfect bliss." So saying he led her back to poor Leonora's bedside, and kneeling beside her, prayed earnestly that strength might be given to him, and to the wretched mother, to bow patiently to the

Divine dispensation, and to be able to say with heartfelt sincerity, " Thy will be done."

And so the dreary hours passed away, and no sleep visited the inmates of the Manor. All kept watch, and waited for the end, save Meredith, who was so completely prostrated by the severe wound and loss of blood, that he readily succumbed to the effects of the composing draught, administered to him by Dr. Quin, and in a deep, dreamless, sleep, his naturally strong, healthy frame, speedily recovered from the shock it had received. Yet another day, and Leonora still lay to all appearance insensible, so still and white she looked, that, but for the faint breath that clouded the glass when held to her lips, those around her, would have believed that all was over. Tom and his wife had arrived, and the former had gone up to Meredith, whilst Meg, once again, took her place at Leonora's bedside, and forced Ellen, who had watched all night, to take a few hours' repose. But nothing would induce the old Marchesa to leave her daughter; praying and fasting, she knelt beside her, stifling the heavy sobs that rose in her throat, and anxiously watching for a sign of returning consciousness. So the day passed, and the shades of evening again gathered around, when a change passed over the features of the sufferer; suddenly her eyes opened, and a faint smile of recognition parted her lips, as she saw the well-known face of her old attendant bending affectionately over her. Dr. Quin had passed the night and day at the Manor, and now, hastily preparing a cordial that he hoped would give his patient strength to speak, he gently raised her, whilst Meg administered it, and then at the doctor's request, placed pillows to prop her up in bed. A fictitious strength was thus for a short time vouchsafed to the dying woman, and looking feebly around, she saw her mother, and kindly held out her hand, which was grasped fervently by the poor Marchesa, as she covered it with kisses, whilst Meg quickly rang the bell, and told the attendants to summon Sir Charles, Dr. Grey, and Ellen, and the Catholic Priest.

"Dear mother," were Leonora's first words, "don't weep for me; it is happier, better so. I go to a brighter land, where no sorrow or evil can reach me; the Holy Virgin has answered my prayers; I feel my sins are pardoned in Heaven, and I die in peace."

"My darling," sobbed the poor mother, "can you, will you forgive me? I have ruined your happiness, and have killed you," she added, as she threw her arms round her.

Leonora kissed her, and whispered that all was forgiven, and then asked for Tony and Sir Charles. As she uttered the last words the Baronet, followed by Dr. Grey, entered, and tenderly placing his arms round his dying wife, pressed her fondly to his heart as in the days of yore, before sin and distrust had come between them. "Dear Charles," she murmured, as she looked fondly into his face; "I am dying. Will you not say a word of love to me? tell me you forgive all before I pass the threshold, from which there is no return? Think of me again as the young innocent girl whom you married, and say once more, you love me, before I go."

Lower and lower the Squire bent his head, till his breath mingled with hers, and he kissed her fondly on the lips, and replied in low fervent tones, "May God bless you, Leonora, and may He so deal with me in my last hour, as I now fully and freely forgive you, and love you with all my soul and strength."

"Tony and Luigi," she feebly whispered, "let them come." Evidently the sight of the poor child's corpse, that had hastened her death, had passed from her memory, during the long hours of insensibility, and the doctor signed to all around not to remind her. "They will be here presently," he said, "I have sent to seek them."

"It will be too late," said Leonora faintly,

as another change passed over her face, and then a smile of heavenly peace and radiance seemed to settle on her features, as she clung with weak caressing arms to her husband's breast, and said, "Dearest do not weep for me, for I am happy now. In this soft hour, I feel the presence of the Eternal that is within us, and that our parting will only be for a short space; a brief span, followed by everlasting communion and joy." Her voice seemed like a voice from another world, lulling the spirit from the cares and griefs of this, and thrilled the heart of each around her bed, with an inexpressible power.

The Priest solemnly said the prayers for the dying, as, apparently wearied out by her emotions, and the fatigue of speaking, Leonora closed her eyes and slowly sank lower on her pillows. One quivering sigh; one gasp for the fleeting breath; one gentle smile to the poor mother, who wept so bitterly beside her, and Leonora glided into death, as a solitary star, like the hope of the future, broke forth upon the growing gloom of her chamber, and shed a faint twinkling ray upon the earth.

THE END.

PRINTED BY
KELLY AND CO., GATE STREET, LINCOLN'S INN FIELDS,
AND KINGSTON-ON-THAMES.

31, Southampton Street, Strand,
London, W.C.

March, 1889.

WHITE & CO.'S
LIST OF
PUBLICATIONS.

Novels at all Libraries in Town and Country.

BEAUTIFUL JIM.
By JOHN STRANGE WINTER, Author of "Bootles' Baby," "Mignon's Husband," "Bootles' Children," &c. 2 Vols.
"A story that has the merits of movement and liveliness."—*Academy*.
"'Beautiful Jim' is as fresh and engaging a work as this charming writer has produced, while the structure of its plot has a peculiar strength which adds much to the effect of the story as a whole.—*Scotsman*.

PURPLE AND FINE LINEN.
By Mrs. ALEXANDER FRASER. 3 Vols.

SEVERED TIES.
By Mrs. HENRY WYLDE. 3 Vols. (March.)

THE MASTER OF RATHKELLY.
By HAWLEY SMART. 2 Vols.

LANDING A PRIZE.
A Novel. By Mrs. EDWARD KENNARD, Author of "The Girl in the Brown Habit," "Killed in the Open," &c. 3 Vols.

ON CIRCUMSTANTIAL EVIDENCE.
By FLORENCE MARRYAT, Author of "My Sister the Actress,' "Facing the Footlights," &c. 3 Vols. (April.)

THIS WICKED WORLD.
By Mrs. H. LOVETT CAMERON, Author of "In a Grass Country," "A North Country Maid," &c. 3 Vols. (2nd Edition.

HER LAST RUN.
By the Honble. Mrs. WALTER R. D. FORBES (Eveline Michell Farwell), Author of "Fingers and Fortune," "The Man in Cords," &c. 2 Vols.

LONG ODDS.
By HAWLEY SMART. 3 Vols.

A DISTRACTING GUEST.
By Mrs. ROBERT JOCELYN. 2 Vols.

THE HON. MRS. VEREKER.
By the Author of "Molly Bawn," "Phyllis," &c. 2 Vols.

F. V. WHITE & Co., 31, Southampton Street, Strand.

F. V. WHITE & Co's Publications.

THE WORKS OF JOHN STRANGE WINTER.

UNIFORM IN STYLE AND PRICE.

Each in Paper Covers, 1/-; Cloth, 1/6. At all Booksellers & Bookstalls

MY POOR DICK.
(4th Edition.) Illustrated by MAURICE GREIFFENHAGEN.

BOOTLES' CHILDREN.
(5th Edition.) Illustrated by J. BERNARD PARTRIDGE.

"John Strange Winter is never more thoroughly at home than when delineating the characters of children, and everyone will be delighted with the dignified Madge and the quaint Pearl. The book is mainly occupied with the love affairs of Terry (the soldier servant who appears in many of the preceding books), but the children buzz in and out of its pages much as they would come in and out of a room in real life, pervading and brightening the house in which they dwell."—*Leicester Daily Post.*

THE CONFESSIONS OF A PUBLISHER.

"The much discussed question of the relations between a publisher and his clients furnishes Mr. John Strange Winter with material for one of the brightest tales of the season. Abel Drinkwater's autobiography is written from a humorous point of view; yet here, as elsewhere, 'many a true word is spoken in jest,' and in the conversations of the publisher and his too ingenuous son facts come to light that are worthy of the attention of aspirants to literary fame."—*Morning Post.*

MIGNON'S HUSBAND. (8th Edition.)

"It is a capital love story, full of high spirits, and written in a dashing style that will charm the most melancholy of readers into hearty enjoyment of its fun."—*Scotsman.*

"The name of John Strange Winter is enough to tell the reader that 'Mignon's Husband' is a brisk, lively tale, with a little pathos but more fun."—*Graphic.*

THAT IMP. 7th Edition.)

"Barrack life is abandoned for the nonce, and the author of 'Bootles' Baby' introduces readers to a country home replete with every comfort, and containing men and women whose acquaintanceship we can only regret can never blossom into friendship."—*Whitehall Review.*

"This charming little book is bright and breezy, and has the ring of supreme truth about it."—*Vanity Fair.*

MIGNON'S SECRET. (11th Edition.)

"In 'Mignon's Secret' Mr. Winter has supplied a continuation to the never-to-be-forgotten 'Bootles' Baby.' . . . The story is gracefully and touchingly told."—*John Bull.*

"A clever little story. . . . It is lightly touched, and has somewhat a tragic termination. It is easy to imagine we have not seen the last of 'Mignon' yet by a long way."—*Punch.*

F. V. WHITE & Co., 31, Southampton Street, Strand.

THE WORKS OF JOHN STRANGE WINTER—*(continued).*

ON MARCH. (6th Edition.)

"This short story is characterised by Mr. Winter's customary truth in detail, humour, and pathos."—*Academy.*

"By publishing 'On March,' Mr J. S. Winter has added another little gem to his well-known store of regimental sketches. The story is written with humour and a deal of feeling."—*Army & Navy Gazette.*

IN QUARTERS. (7th Edition.)

"'In Quarters' is one of those rattling tales of soldiers' life which the public have learned to thoroughly appreciate."—*The Graphic.*

"The author of 'Bootles' Baby' gives us here another story of military life, which few have better described."—*British Quarterly Review.*

ARMY SOCIETY; Life in a Garrison Town.

Cloth, 6/-; also in Picture Boards, 2/-. (8th Edition.)

"This discursive story, dealing with life in a garrison town, is full of pleasant 'go' and movement which has distinguished 'Bootles' Baby,' 'Pluck,' or in fact a majority of some half-dozen novelettes which the author has submitted to the eyes of railway bookstall patronisers."—*Daily Telegraph.*

"The strength of the book lies in its sketches of life in a garrison town, which are undeniably clever. . . . It is pretty clear that Mr. Winter draws from life."—*St. James's Gazette.*

GARRISON GOSSIP, Gathered in Blankhampton.

(A Sequel to "ARMY SOCIETY.") Cloth, 2/6; also in Picture Boards, 2/-. (4th Edition.)

"'Garrison Gossip' may fairly rank with 'Cavalry Life,' and the various other books with which Mr. Winter has so agreeably beguiled our leisure hours."—*Saturday Review.*

"The novel fully maintains the reputation which its author has been fortunate enough to gain in a special line of his own."—*Graphic.*

A SIEGE BABY. Cloth, 2/6; Picture boards, 2/-

"The story which gives its title to this new sheaf of stories by the popular author of 'Bootles' Baby' is a very touching and pathetic one. . . . Amongst the other stories, the one entitled, 'Out of the Mists' is, perhaps, the best written, although the tale of true love it embodies comes to a most melancholy ending."—*County Gentlemen.*

BEAUTIFUL JIM.

Cloth Gilt, 2/6. (April.)

F. V. WHITE & Co., 31, Southampton Street, Strand.

F. V. WHITE & Co.'s Publications. 5

MRS. EDWARD KENNARD'S SPORTING NOVELS.
At all Booksellers and Bookstalls.

A CRACK COUNTY.
Cloth gilt, 2/6.

THE GIRL IN THE BROWN HABIT.
Cloth gilt, 2/6; Picture Boards, 2/-. (4th Edition.)

"'Nell Fitzgerald' is an irreproachable heroine, full of gentle womanliness, and rich in all virtues that make her kind estimable. Mrs. Kennard's work is marked by high tone as well as vigorous narrative, and sportsmen, when searching for something new and beguiling for a wet day or spell of frost, can hardly light upon anything better than these fresh and picturesque hunting stories of Mrs. Kennard's."—*Daily Telegraph.*

KILLED IN THE OPEN.
Cloth gilt, 2/6; Picture Boards, 2/-. (3rd Edition.)

"It is in truth a very good love story set in a framework of hounds and horses but one that could be read with pleasure independently of any such attractions."—*Fortnightly Review.*

"'Killed in the Open' is a very superior sort of hunting novel indeed."—*Graphic.*

STRAIGHT AS A DIE.
Cloth gilt, 2/6; Picture Boards, 2/-. (3rd Edition.)

"If you like sporting novels I can recommend to you Mrs. Kennard's 'Straight as a Die.'"—*Truth.*

"'Straight as a Die' is well and pleasantly written."—*Graphic.*

"Mrs. Edward Kennard can write, and write well. Her descriptions of country life are many of them admirable, and her story will be read to the end. Some of the love passages between Dulcie and Bob are full of beauty and pathos."—*Pictorial World.*

A REAL GOOD THING.
Cloth gilt, 2/6. Also Picture Boards, 2/-. (5th Edition.)

"There are some good country scenes and country spins in 'A Real Good Thing.' The hero, poor old Hopkins, is a strong character."—*Academy.*

"The title of this novel betrays the order to which it belongs, and a very lively, readable specimen it is. The writer is evidently an enthusiast in the matter of hunting, and there is always something very exhilarating in such descriptions as are here to be found of excellent runs with horn and hound and gallant horse, with brave and stalwart men, and with pretty women quite as brave."—*St. James's Gazette.*

TWILIGHT TALES. (*Illustrated.* Cloth gilt, 2/6.)
BY THE SAME AUTHOR.
In Paper Covers, 1/-; Cloth, 1/6. The Second Edition of

A GLORIOUS GALLOP.

F. V. WHITE & Co., 31, Southampton Street, Strand.

HAWLEY SMART'S SPORTING NOVELS.

At all Booksellers and Bookstalls.

THE MASTER OF RATHKELLY.
Cloth gilt, 2/6. (April.)

THE OUTSIDER.
Cloth gilt, 2/6; Picture Boards, 2/-. (4th Edition.)

"Since the deaths of Surtees and Whyte Melville, Captain Hawley Smart has worthily held his place at the head of those writers who devote themselves to sporting subjects . . . his readers know precisely what to expect when they take up one of his books, and they are never disappointed."—*Saturday Review.*

BY THE SAME AUTHOR.

Each in Paper Cover, 1/-; Cloth, 1/6.

THE LAST COUP.

THE PRIDE OF THE PADDOCK.

CLEVERLY WON.

THE HONOURABLE MRS. FETHERSTONHAUCH'S NEW NOVEL.

DREAM FACES. Cloth, 2/6.
By the Author of "Kilcorran," "Robin Adair," &c.

BRET HARTE'S NEW NOVEL.
Cloth, 2/6.

THE CRUSADE OF THE EXCELSIOR.
By the Author of "The Luck of Roaring Camp," &c.

"As a sketcher of the life of the Far West he is still unrivalled. . . . Mr. Bret Harte's readers will greatly enjoy the amusing account of the travellers' life at the Mexican outpost, and the very clever way in which at last the castaways are extricated. In this story the author shows a faculty of invention and a literary tact so noteworthy that we may even venture to expect another romance as superior in permanent value to the delightful crusade of the 'Excelsior' as the latter is to its lengthy predecessor 'Gabriel Conroy.'"—*Academy.*

SIR RANDAL ROBERT'S NEW SPORTING NOVEL.

CURB AND SNAFFLE. Cloth gilt, 2/6.
By the Author of "In the Shires," &c.

F. V. WHITE & Co., 31, Southampton Street, Strand.

F. V. WHITE & Co.'s Publications.

MRS. H. LOVETT CAMERON'S NOVELS.

At all Booksellers and Bookstalls.

IN A GRASS COUNTRY.

A Story of Love and Sport.) (7th Edition.) Cloth gilt, 2/6; Picture Boards, 2/-.

"We turn with pleasure to the green covers of 'In a Grass Country.' The three heroines are charming each in her own way. It is well sketched, full of character, with sharp observations of men and women—not too hard on anybody—a clear story carefully written, and therefore easily read. . . . recommended."—*Punch.*

"When the days are short and there is an hour or two to be disposed of indoors before dressing time, one is glad to be able to recommend a good and amusing novel. 'In a Grass Country' may be said to come under this description."—*Saturday Review.*

A NORTH COUNTRY MAID.

(3rd Edition.) Cloth, 2/6; Picture Boards, 2/-.

A DEAD PAST.

(3rd Edition.) Cloth, 2/6; Picture Boards, 2/-.

A DEVOUT LOVER. Cloth, 2/6.

"Without doubt, one of Mrs. Lovett Cameron's best and prettiest stories. The character of Rose de Brefour is admirably drawn. . . . Mrs. Lovett Cameron deserves great credit for having made a good woman interesting."—*Ladies' Pictorial.*

THE COST OF A LIE.

Cloth gilt, 2/6.

BY THE SAME AUTHOR.

Each in Paper Cover, 1/-; Cloth, 1/6.

NECK OR NOTHING.

". . . It is pleasant, easy reading, and the characters act in a way one can understand."—*Saturday Review.*

". . . is really very bright and readable from first to last."—*Academy.*

". . . is a capital story of hunting and love-making combined. . . . Nothing prettier or more natural has been written for some time than the scene in which Lucy Netterville betrays her cherished secret with such happy results."—*Pictorial World.*

THE MADNESS OF MARRIAGE.

"Mrs. Lovett Cameron's books are never devoid of merit. . . . The interest in Daisy Carew's fate is well sustained. . . ."—*Morning Post.*

F. V. WHITE & Co., 31, Southampton Street, Strand.

MRS. ALEXANDER'S NOVELS.

At all Booksellers and Bookstalls.

A FALSE SCENT.
Paper Cover, 1/-; Cloth, 1/6.

BY WOMAN'S WIT.
(3rd Edition.) Cloth, 2/6; Picture Boards, 2/-.

"Mrs. Alexander deserves credit for keeping her readers mystified for some time in the matter of Mrs. Ruthven's rubies. . . . How the widow's wit discovers the treachery of the man she loves in spite of it; how she avenges herself, and the terrible straits Nora is involved in for a season, when she has accepted the wrong man, because the right man has been slow to declare himself; and how all ends well for her and her gentle stepmother, not to mention the old shikari whom she weds, is written in Mrs. Alexander's book, and very readably."—*Athenæum*.

> "In Mrs. Alexander's tale
> Much art she clearly shows
> In keeping dark the mystery
> Until the story's close!"—*Punch*.

MONA'S CHOICE. Cloth, 2/6.

"Mrs. Alexander has written a novel quite worthy of her."—*Athenæum*.

". . . it is pleasant and unaffected."—*Saturday Review*.

"The story is pleasantly told, and some of the subsidiary characters are specially good. Mr. Craig, Mona's uncle, is indeed a triumph of truthful and humorous delineation, and we think that on the whole 'Mona's Choice' must be considered Mrs. Alexander's best novel."—*Spectator*.

"RITA'S" NEW NOVELS.

Each in Paper Cover, 1/-; Cloth, 1/6. At all Booksellers & Bookstalls.

THE MYSTERY OF A TURKISH BATH.
(2nd Edition.)

"Every fresh piece of work which 'Rita' publishes, shows an increase of power, and a decided advance on the last. The booklet contains some very smart writing indeed."—*Whitehall Review*.

"'The Mystery of a Turkish Bath' has a well-wrought out plot of slightly sensational interest, and is written with this author's well-known grace of style."—*Scotsman*.

THE SEVENTH DREAM. A Romance.

". . . is a powerful and interesting study in weird effects of fiction. It will hold the close attention of its readers from first to last, and keep them entertained with changing sensations of wonder."—*Scotsman*.

F. V. WHITE & Co., 31, Southampton Street, Strand.

F. V. WHITE & Co.'s Publications.

NEW ONE SHILLING NOVEL.
By CURTIS YORKE,
ENTITLED
THE MYSTERY OF BELGRAVE SQUARE.
Cloth, 1/6.

POPULAR WORKS AT ALL BOOKSELLERS AND BOOKSTALLS.

By SAMUEL LAING.
A MODERN ZOROASTRIAN.
By the Author of "Modern Science and Modern Thought," "A Sporting Quixote," &c.

1 Vol. *Cloth*, 2/6.   (*Second Edition.*)

By W. H. DAVENPORT ADAMS.
CELEBRATED ENGLISHWOMEN OF THE VICTORIAN ERA.
By the Author of "England on the Sea," &c.

1 Vol. *Cloth*, 2/6.

By PERCY THORPE.
HISTORY OF JAPAN.
1 Vol. *Cloth*, 3/6.

F. V. WHITE & Co., 31, Southampton Street, Strand.

"SELECT" NOVELS.

Crown 8vo., Clot 2s. 6d. each.
AT ALL BOOKSELLERS AND BOOKSTALLS.

BY FLORENCE MARRYAT.

1. THE HEIR PRESUMPTIVE.
2. THE HEART OF JANE WARNER.
3. UNDER THE LILIES AND ROSES.
4. HER WORLD AGAINST A LIE.
5. FACING THE FOOTLIGHTS.

BY ANNIE THOMAS (Mrs. Pender Cudlip).

6. HER SUCCESS.
7. FRIENDS AND LOVERS.
8. JENIFER.
9. KATE VALLIANT.
10. ALLERTON TOWERS.

BY LADY CONSTANCE HOWARD.

11. MATED WITH A CLOWN.
12. MOLLIE DARLING.
13. ONLY A VILLAGE MAIDEN.

BY MRS. HOUSTOUN.

Author of "Recommended to Mercy."

14. BARBARA'S WARNING.

BY MRS. ALEXANDER FRASER.

15. A PROFESSIONAL BEAUTY.

F. V. WHITE & CO., 31, Southampton Street, Strand.

"SELECT" NOVELS—(continued).

BY HARRIETT JAY.
16 A MARRIAGE OF CONVENIENCE.

BY IZA DUFFUS HARDY.
17 LOVE, HONOUR, AND OBEY.
18 NOT EASILY JEALOUS.
19 ONLY A LOVE STORY.

BY JEAN MIDDLEMASS.
20 POISONED ARROWS.

BY MRS. H. LOVETT CAMERON.
21 A NORTH COUNTRY MAID
22 A DEAD PAST.

BY LADY VIOLET GREVILLE.
23 KEITH'S WIFE.

BY NELLIE FORTESCUE HARRISON.
Author of "So Runs My Dream."
24 FOR ONE MAN'S PLEASURE.

BY EDMUND LEATHES.
25 THE ACTOR'S WIFE.

F. V. WHITE & CO., 31, Southampton Street, Strand.

F. V. WHITE & Co.'s Publications.

"POPULAR" NOVELS.
Picture Boards, 2s. each.
AT ALL BOOKSELLERS AND BOOKSTALLS.

1 GARRISON GOSSIP. By JOHN STRANGE WINTER, Author of "A Siege Baby," "In Quarters," "On March," "Mignon's Secret," "That Imp," "Mignon's Husband," &c. (Fourth Edition.)

2 ARMY SOCIETY; Or, Life in a Garrison Town. By the same Author. (Eighth Edition.)

3 THE OUTSIDER. By HAWLEY SMART, Author of "The Pride of the Paddock," "Cleverly Won," "Bad to Beat," "Lightly Lost," &c.

4 BY WOMAN'S WIT. By Mrs. ALEXANDER, Author of "Mona's Choice," "The Wooing O't," "The Executor," "Admiral's Ward," &c.

5 THE GIRL IN THE BROWN HABIT. By Mrs. EDWARD KENNARD, Author of "Straight as a Die," "Twilight Tales," "A Real Good Thing," "A Glorious Gallop," "A Crack County," &c.

6 KILLED IN THE OPEN. By the same Author.

7 STRAIGHT AS A DIE. By Mrs. EDWARD KENNARD, Author of "A Real Good Thing," &c.

8 IN A GRASS COUNTRY: A Story of Love and Sport. By Mrs. H. LOVETT CAMERON, (Seventh Edition.)

9 A NORTH COUNTRY MAID. By the same Author.

10 A DEAD PAST. By the same Author.

F. V. WHITE & Co., 31, Southampton Street, Strand.

"POPULAR" NOVELS—(continued).

11 POISONED ARROWS. By JEAN MIDDLEMASS, Author of "Wild Georgie," "Dandy."

12 ONLY A LOVE STORY By IZA DUFFUS HARDY, Author of "Love, Honour, and Obey."

13 THE HEART OF JANE WARNER. By FLORENCE MARRYAT, Author of "Facing the Footlights," "Her World against a Lie," "The Heir Presumptive," "My own Child," &c.

14 UNDER THE LILIES AND ROSES. By the same Author.

15 KATE VALLIANT. By ANNIE THOMAS (Mrs. Pender Cudlip), Author of "Her Success."

16 KEITH'S WIFE. By Lady VIOLET GREVILLE, Author of "Zoe: A Girl of Genius," "Creatures of Clay."

17 MATED WITH A CLOWN. By Lady CONSTANCE HOWARD, Author of "Only a Village Maiden," "Mollie Darling."

18 NOT EASILY JEALOUS. By IZA DUFFUS HARDY, Author of "Love, Honour, and Obey," &c.

19 FOR ONE MAN'S PLEASURE. By NELLIE FORTESCUE HARRISON, Author of "So Runs My Dream," &c.

20 THE CRUSADE OF "THE EXCELSIOR." By BRET HARTE.

21 A SIEGE BABY. By JOHN STRANGE WINTER.

F. V. WHITE & CO., 31, Southampton Street, Strand.

ONE SHILLING NOVELS.

In Paper Cover.

THOSE MARKED * CAN ALSO BE OBTAINED IN CLOTH (1/6).
At all Booksellers and Bookstalls.

1 *MY POOR DICK. (Fourth Edition.) By JOHN STRANGE WINTER, Author of "Bootles' Baby," "Houp La," &c. (With Illustrations by MAURICE GREIFFENHAGEN.)

2 *BOOTLES' CHILDREN. (Fifth Edition.) By the same Author. (With Illustrations by J. BERNARD PARTRIDGE.)

3 *THE CONFESSIONS OF A PUBLISHER. By the same Author.

4 *MIGNON'S HUSBAND. (Eighth Edition.) By the same Author.

5 *THAT IMP. (Seventh Edition.) By the same Author.

6 *MIGNON'S SECRET. (Eleventh Edition.) By the same Author.

7 *ON MARCH. (Sixth Edition.) By the same Author.

8 *IN QUARTERS. (Seventh Edition.) By the same Author.

9 *A GLORIOUS GALLOP. (Second Edition.) By Mrs. EDWARD KENNARD, Author of "The Girl in the Brown Habit," "A Real Good Thing," &c.

10 *THE MYSTERY OF A TURKISH BATH. (Second Edition.) By "Rita," Author of "Dame Durden," "Sheba," "My Lord Conceit," &c.

11 *THE SEVENTH DREAM. A Romance. By the same Author.

12 *THE PRIDE OF THE PADDOCK. By HAWLEY SMART, Author of "The Outsider," "The Master of Rathkelly," &c.

F. V. WHITE & CO., 31, Southampton Street, Strand.

ONE SHILLING NOVELS —(continued).

13 *CLEVERLY WON. By HAWLEY SMART.
14 *A MILLIONAIRE OF ROUGH AND READY. By BRET HARTE, Author of "The Luck of Roaring Camp," &c.
15 *DEVIL'S FORD. By BRET HARTE.
16 *NECK OR NOTHING: A Hunting Story. By Mrs. H. LOVETT CAMERON, Author of "In a Grass Country," &c. (Second Edition.)
17 *THE MADNESS OF MARRIAGE. By Mrs. H. LOVETT CAMERON.
18 *THE FASHION OF THIS WORLD. By HELEN MATHERS, Author of "Comin' thro' the Rye," &c.
19 *A PLAYWRIGHT'S DAUGHTER. By Mrs. ANNIE EDWARDES, Author of "Archie Lovell, &c.
20 NO MEDIUM. By ANNIE THOMAS (Mrs. Pender Cudlip), Author of "Her Success," &c.
21 A MOMENT OF MADNESS. By FLORENCE MARRYAT, Author of "My Sister the Actress," &c.
22 SAVED IN TIME. By Mrs. HOUSTOUN, Author of "Recommended to Mercy," &c.
23 EVERY INCH A WOMAN. By Mrs. HOUSTOUN.
24 A PAUPER PEER. By Major ARTHUR GRIFFITHS, Author of "Fast and Loose," &c.
25 *THE WESTHORPE MYSTERY. By IZA DUFFUS HARDY, Author of "Love, Honour, and Obey," &c.
26 *STORIES OF "THE WORLD." (Reprinted by Permission.)
27 TWO BLACK PEARLS. By MARIE CONNOR, Author of "A Morganatic Marriage," "Beauty's Queen," &c.

F. V. WHITE & Co., 31, Southampton Street, Strand.

PRICE ONE SHILLING.

London Society:

ESTABLISHED 1862.

A MONTHLY MAGAZINE

of light and amusing literature by the most popular authors of the day.

TERMS OF SUBSCRIPTION:
PAYABLE IN ADVANCE.

TWELVE MONTHS, SENT POST FREE . . . . 12s.
DO., INCLUDING THE SUMMER NUMBER AND
      CHRISTMAS ANNUAL . . . . 14s.

OPINIONS OF THE PRESS.

" Readers who like to be amused should take in " London Society " . . .
" London Society " is a good shillingsworth."—*Lady's Pictorial.*

" This attractive magazine is remarkable for variety of subject and excellence of its light literature."—*Public Opinion.*

" Full of the light and amusing literature it professes to supply."—*Literary World.*

" It is bright, interesting, and a perfect mine of light and amusing literature. It is ably conducted, and should enjoy an ever increasing circulation."—*Grantham Times.*

All communications to be addressed to the Editor of " *London Society.*"

F. V. WHITE & CO.,
31, SOUTHAMPTON STREET, STRAND, LONDON, W.C.

www.ingramcontent.com/pod-product-compliance
Lightning Source LLC
Chambersburg PA
CBHW032123230426

43672CB00009B/1844